THOMAS HARRISON
Georgian Architect of Chester and Lancaster
1744–1829

JOHN CHAMPNESS

Centre for North-West Regional Studies
University of Lancaster
2005
Series Editor: Jean Turnbull

THOMAS HARRISON
Georgian Architect of Chester and Lancaster
1744–1829

This volume is the 52nd in a series of Occasional Papers published by the
Centre for North-West Regional Studies at the University of Lancaster

Designed, typeset, printed and bound by
JW Arrowsmith Ltd, Bristol

British Library Cataloguing in-Publication Data
A CIP calalogue entry for this book is available from the British Library

ISBN 1-86220-169-2

The publishers gratefully acknowledge grants towards this publication
from Dr Philip Welch and The Chester Civic Trust.

Contents

Acknowledgements

I could not have written a work such as this, which deals with some 60 buildings, without help from many other people. I would not even have contemplated it, if the Editorial Board of the Centre for North-West Regional Studies had not invited me to do so, and I owe them special thanks for their invitation, and their administrative and editorial support.

I am also very grateful for the unstinted help, received from the staff at the Record Offices in Cheshire, Derbyshire, Lancashire and Shropshire; at the Chester Heritage Centre, and the National Monuments Records in Edinburgh and Swindon; the Word and Image Department of the Victoria and Albert Museum, and the British Library; and in the libraries at Chester, Derby, Lancaster, Manchester, and Oxford Brookes University.

I have been overwhelmed by the kindness and generosity of owners and curators, who did not know me but made me welcome, and of other architects, engineers and scholars – plus friends (in all three camps) – who have shared their information and corrected many of my mistakes. (For those, which remain, I alone bear the responsibility.) I am deeply grateful to them all and, to avoid invidious distinctions, name them here in the alphabetical order of their surnames: Clive Allen, Valerie Anderson, Susan Ashworth, David Aukland, Robert Bargery, Michael Bidnell, Pam Bosworth, Peter Boughton, Susan Bourne, Katie Cavanagh, Graham Cliffe, Trevor Clifford, Howard Colvin, John Cousins, Ian Cumming, Robin Darwall-Smith, Peter De Figueiredo, Mike Derbyshire, Denys Doxat-Pratt, Mac Dunsmore, Eva Edwards, Melinda Elder, the Earl of Elgin, Graham Fisher, Stephen Gardner, Emmeline Garnett, Margaret Garnett, Bernard Gayle, Christine Goodier, Beverley and Sylvia Griffiths, Michael Harris, Jane Hatcher, Jennifer Holt, George Howson, Jackie Hughes, Gwyneth Jones, Hilary Jones, Philippa Jones, Judith Lawson, Jenny Loveridge, Pam Lynch, Alan McAllester, Bobbie and Angela McAlpine, Marion McClintock, Ruth McKew, Roy McLeod, The President and Fellows of Magdalen College, Oxford, Emma Marigliano, Guy Myddelton, Ann Nash, Peter Norris, Howard and Eileen Oldroyd, Anne Pinder, James Price, James Rainy-Brown, Peter Richards, Mike Roberts, John Martin Robinson, Stephen Sartin, Ian Serjeant, Iain and Su Sharp, Dorothy Simpson, Colin Stansfield, Jane Steele, Duncan Steaton, Craig Thornber, Jean Turnbull, Kathleen and Lawrence Walker, Chris Wedge, the Earl and Countess of Wemyss, Andrew White, Mark White, Roger White, Ian Whittle, Eric Wilkinson, Ian Wilson, Susan Wilson, Michael Winstanley, Mark Wyatt; and, last but certainly not least, my wife, Doreen, who has loyally supported and lovingly tolerated me during the last 18 months, and for half my lifetime before then.

John Champness
Lancaster
May Day 2005

Notes and References

An asterisk or a dagger within brackets [*] [†] indicates a footnote at the bottom of the page.

Superscript numbers [7] refer to the references to each chapter, printed at the end of the text.

Captions

The date on a caption is the date of the image and not of the building.

Access

Where Harrison's surviving buildings stand outside town centres, I have given – in Appendix A – a rough indication of their position by means of the number of the current O.S Landranger map and of the National Grid square, in which they appear. For example, Skerton Bridge – his first major work – is marked on OS map number 97 in the square 47.62, so its position is here expressed as at 97/47.62.

A dozen or so of these buildings are private houses or private offices and therefore not open to the public. I have tried to avoid all doubt on this matter, by stating unambiguously when buildings are private or stand in private grounds. In some cases they may be visible from a public highway, but in all cases their interiors are not accessible to visitors.

Illustrations

Frontispiece: Thomas Harrison, 1820 by H. Wyatt.
Reproduced by permission of Cheshire and Chester Archives and Local Studies.

Introduction

There are few 'north-western' architects whose names mean anything outside the north west. The dynasty of Paley and Austin – the subject of another monograph, published by the Centre for North-West Regional Studies – are certainly among them; and the Websters of Kendal must count with them, especially after the publication of Angus Taylor's book in 2004. Perhaps Richard Gillow does too, though his reputation hangs more on his work as a furniture designer. The only other north-western architect, who is a candidate for national recognition, is Thomas Harrison 'of Chester', whom Sir Nikolaus Pevsner described as 'a local architect whose work is as good as that of any in London'.[1] (His work in Liverpool and Manchester is also highly praised by Joseph Sharples and Clare Hartwell respectively in their recent Pevsner Architectural Guides to those cities.) Sir John Summerson rated him as 'a man of outstanding ability', but then, two pages later, after praising his works at Chester Castle highly, added the significant qualification: 'Many of his later works are very tame, and one feels that his isolation in a provincial centre may have prevented him from reaching the standard, which his abilities ought to have made attainable. On the other hand, it may be proper to class him with Robert Mylne, as a man primarily of an engineering bent, whose capacities as an artist were sound but limited'.[2]

It is true that Harrison had something of an engineering bent: his 40 years of professional practice began with a bridge in Lancaster – supposedly, the first in England with a level road deck – and ended with a bridge in Chester – whose stone arch certainly had the longest span in the world. However, he designed much more than bridges – not least most of the buildings now known as the Castle in both Lancaster and Chester. These works alone are enough to secure him an honourable mention in histories of English architecture. However, in addition to these he made designs for half a dozen country houses, a dozen attractive villas, a few churches and public monuments and – a new building type, this – gentlemen's newsrooms and libraries in Chester, Liverpool and Manchester. David Watkin gave him half a page (out of 200) in his history of English architecture and praised him as 'the finest' of the architects who revived the forms of ancient Greek architecture.[3] He gave him, of course, a score of mentions in his book on Regency buildings,[4] but not a word in his larger work on Western architecture. Are we perhaps looking at a man whose work, in Michelin terms, does not justify a special journey but is worth a detour?

Whatever the verdict, an armchair journey to see the works of a Yorkshireman, who trained in Rome and first made his name in Lancaster, but spent the bulk of his working career in Chester, is – I believe – worth the time spent. Harrison was a man who, though he worked a long way from London, was aware of what was happening in contemporary Europe and helped to introduce what is called the Greek Revival into England. His 50 or so surviving works provide windows into the very different world of late Georgian society; many of them are of historical interest, and some are works of real architectural quality.

The main facts of Harrison's life, as of those of every Georgian architect of any consequence, are to be found in the pages of Sir Howard Colvin's monumental and indispensable *Biographical Dictionary of British Architects, 1600–1840*.[5] However, since J. Mordaunt Crook wrote his revelatory articles on Harrison in *Country Life* in 1971,[6] the only detailed studies have been Moira Ockrim's unpublished doctoral thesis, written in 1988,[7] her recent entry on Harrison in the *Oxford Dictionary of National Biography*,[8] and a few articles in specialist journals. I was therefore happy to accept the Centre's invitation to write a monograph on his life and works. Thomas Harrison deserves to be better known.

This work makes few claims to original scholarship. Apart from pulling together what I hope is a coherent and plausible story from Colvin and Ockrim and a host of documentary sources, secondary and primary, my main contribution is to have visited every one of Harrison's surviving buildings and to have noted my reactions on site. These buildings are, of course, the primary source *par excellence*, and I have expanded my notes into the descriptions and appraisals in the text. The works of any architect are influenced by people and by changing fashions, and so I feel that it makes sense to treat them as far as possible in a more or less chronological narrative, with the necessary analysis and critical comment woven in as seamlessly as possible.

I have described all the buildings, which Colvin attributes to Harrison with confidence. I have also described a few more, which in my considered opinion must have been designed by him – although the evidence does not amount to certain proof. One can only attribute a building to an architect with certainty, if documents, like signed drawings or plans or specific invoices, can be shown, or if the attribution is made within a few years of the building's construction by someone who must have known the facts and had no motive to mislead.[(*)] Apart from such cases, one is reduced to

---

[(*)] A problem with Harrison is that no <u>signed</u> drawing or plan has been found; the best that exists is a drawing <u>dated</u>, for example 'Chester, 1 March 1818'. Harrison's last surviving daughter, Anne, gave all of her father's drawings, which she could find in his house, to the

a degree of surmise, based on the similarities of plan or style between a securely attributed building or drawing and another, about which there is doubt. One has to be cautious to the point of serious scepticism: the case for an attribution must be made beyond reasonable doubt, and even then I believe that, without documentary evidence which provides proof, no words stronger than 'almost certain' are justified. A 'probable' attribution is even less secure.

I have written little on Harrison's buildings, which have not survived, unless they are of particular significance. All of these 'lost' buildings have their names printed for the first time in *bold italics*. Since the illustrations are an integral part of this book, I have only devoted more than two or three paragraphs to those of his surviving buildings, which in my view are of particular architectural quality or, if of lesser quality, are nevertheless of major significance in the history of the development of his work. I make no apology for this emphasis on quality: architectural history should be the history of architecture, that is, of buildings of above-average quality. Harrison, like Homer, did occasionally nod, but he was an architect who was at least the equal of any single one of the Paleys, Austins and Websters.

Chester Archaeological, Architectural and Historical Society in 1849. A few others were subsequently found in 1959, before the house was bought by Cheshire County Council. The drawings, which were given by Miss Harrison to the CAAHS, were later given by the Society to the County Council for safekeeping, but have somehow become split between the County Record Office and the Museums Service. As well as a number of Harrison drawings in the hands of the successors of his clients, there are a few in the Grosvenor Museum, Chester, and some in the RIBA Drawings Collection and at the Courtauld Institute of Art. (I have not seen these last two sets with my own eyes.)

CHAPTER ONE

Thomas Harrison: his Origins and Training

Thomas Harrison started his professional career in December 1782 at the age of 38 – somewhat late nowadays, but even more so two centuries ago, when most people did not live beyond 60. What is more, he started with a masterpiece. Skerton Bridge is perhaps the most elegant bridge in Lancashire and became a model for a number of other more famous bridges, including the London Bridge which is now in Arizona. This story does not sound plausible; it is only in Greek mythology that the goddess Athene can spring, fully armed, from the head of her father, Zeus. A mere mortal like Harrison cannot have designed Skerton Bridge without being both gifted and well grounded in the practice of building. And yet, we know next to nothing of his life and training before 1782.[1]

Even the date of his birth is not known. He was born in Richmond, Yorkshire, and was the son of a joiner, also called Thomas Harrison, who had his own business there. He is probably the Thomas Harrison, who was baptised on 7 August 1744. He must have had at least a brother, since he took a nephew, John Harrison, into his practice in the late 1790s. We know that he went to Richmond Grammar School, but can only presume that he served his apprenticeship and followed his father's trade for a time, perhaps dabbling in design work or working on a prestigious site.

He is next mentioned in the records in 1769, when he was sent to study architecture in Rome, at the expense of the major landowner in the Richmond area, Sir Lawrence Dundas, of Aske Hall. The precise details are unclear, but it seems that Dundas asked the Reverend Anthony Temple, the Headmaster of Richmond Grammar School, whether he knew of a former pupil, who would benefit from the opportunity to travel to Rome – presumably as a servant to a party of young gentlemen – and then to study there. Temple suggested a budding artist, George Cuit, but Cuit, the son of a local farmer, was apprehensive about travelling so far, alone and in the company of people above his station in life. He therefore asked whether his friend, Thomas Harrison, could accompany him and share his allowance. Dundas must have been impressed by Harrison's talents – apparently in 'arithmetic, mechanics and drawing' – and agreed to pay for him to study in Rome as well. Cuit returned to England in 1775, a year before Harrison, with a collection of Piranesi etchings, doubtless hoping to make a career in London. However, illness forced him to return to Richmond, where he married and worked with some success for 40 years as a landscape painter.

Such patronage of talented but fairly poor young men was not rare in Georgian England; indeed, it was regarded as a good way for a gentleman to display the resources of his estate or locality, and also as part of his 'paternal' duties towards his tenants or local people generally. By so doing, a gentleman not only helped a talented man to fulfil more of his potential, but also acquired immediate esteem among his peers. He might perhaps be able later to enjoy the respect of a wider public as the man who had spotted the talent and helped it to prosper. Perhaps the most famous such case is that of the architect and furniture-designer, William Kent, another Yorkshireman, who was sent in 1709 to study painting in Italy. There he was patronised by a number of Yorkshire gentlemen and later impressed the Yorkshire nobleman and future leading architect, Lord Burlington.

Sir Lawrence Dundas was so important in the story of Harrison's career that he deserves more than a mere footnote. He was born in 1710 as the son of an Edinburgh woollen draper, who came from an old family of landowning gentry. He soon showed himself to be a shrewd and enterprising businessman, making good use of his family name. He married well too; his wife was Margaret Bruce of Kennet. He was a Whig and, after winning a contract to supply the army of the Duke of Cumberland in 1745, was appointed Commissary-General of the British forces in Flanders and Germany between 1748 and 1759. As such he was responsible for supplying food and forage to the armies of Britain and its allies for much of the Seven Years' War – which allowed him, in typical Georgian fashion, to take a small fortune from the public purse. He was made a baronet in 1762 and bought Aske Hall the following year, to gain control of the 'pocket borough' of Richmond. As well as Aske Hall he owned seven other houses, including what is probably the finest house in the New Town of Edinburgh – Dundas House in St Andrew's Square. He was a discerning patron of the arts. He was the MP for Edinburgh between 1768 and 1770, but never secured the peerage which he coveted. His son, Thomas, was, however, made Baron Dundas in 1794.

It is not difficult to imagine Harrison's excitement at the prospect of studying in Rome. Rome was the Eternal City, the artistic capital of Europe; even the French had accepted this in 1661 by founding their Royal Academy there, where the best young French architects could study further. It was in Rome that he would see all the major surviving works of the architecture of the Romans, which had set the standard and provided the motifs for architects since the time of the Renaissance. It was in Rome that the greatest Italian architects of the last three centuries – Bramante, Michelangelo, Bernini – had created their masterpieces. Among the major Italian architects, only Andrea Palladio had not practised in Rome, but he had measured most of the Roman monuments, and, thanks to the enthusiasm of Lord Burlington in the 1730s, his learned interpretation of the architecture of Ancient Rome and his elegant and restrained buildings came to form the basis of what contemporaries called the 'Palladian rules' for design.[*]

We do not know by which route or in whose company Harrison and Cuit travelled to Italy in 1769. Harrison stayed in Rome for about seven years and studied, as a number of British architects had done, and were to do, at the Accademia di San Luca (St Luke). This had been founded in 1593, to provide free instruction in painting and sculpture, and civil and military architecture. [Figure 1] In Harrison's time, it stood near the church of SS. Luca e Martina, a stone's throw away from the half-buried triumphal arch built for Septimius Severus at the western end of the Roman Forum: where better to study?

We do not know how Harrison spent his time in Rome, but he certainly made drawings of many of the ruins of Roman temples there, since a number of these still exist in the Cheshire Record Office.[2] He also measured Trajan's Column – of which some drawings, annotated in Italian, survive at the CRO.[3] He was still very impressed by the Column 40 years later, according to the young architect, Charles Cockerell, who had seen some of Harrison's papers and quoted them in his diary in July 1818. Cockerell noted that Harrison had been overawed, not so much by the artistry of the spiralling picture-sequence portraying the Roman army's campaigns, as by the masons' skill in creating the 98-foot column, and by the sheer size of the 21 hollowed-out round blocks, from which its base, shaft and capital were built. In contrast to Trajan's Column, Harrison had regarded Wren's much taller Monument to the Great Fire of London as no more than 'a pile of stones not to be numbered'.[4] This awed fascination with the sheer massiveness of stone and a concern to emphasise both it and the technical skills of the masons' craft are features, which can be seen in all of Harrison's major buildings.

---

[*] 'Palladian' is the only one of the stylistic labels, now stuck by art historians onto Georgian buildings, which the Georgians used themselves; it is the only one, therefore, which I shall employ. Lord Burlington was a man of great influence, and the 'rules' were closely followed by any architect, who was anxious not to appear uncouth as well as ignorant. They applied primarily to the design of country houses – then the model for any building of significance. Very simply, they laid down that reception rooms should be on the first floor (which was called by the Italian term, the *piano nobile*), above a ground floor for family rooms and a few service rooms. The ground floor was always faced with 'rusticated' masonry, in which the joints between every stone were emphasised, whereas the *piano nobile* and the lower 'chamber floor' – which give rise to the phrase 'a two-and-a-half storey façade' – were faced with smoothly finished stonework called ashlar. External decoration was restrained, and normally limited to a portico with columns and a pediment in the centre of the *piano nobile*. Most service rooms were provided in the wings, which stretched out to either side, often ending in taller pavilions. The most easily visible example in Lancaster of such a format is provided by the Bridge Houses at the end of Skerton Bridge; in Cheshire by Tabley House.

He is thought to have lived in the area of the Piazza di Spagna – known then as the 'English ghetto' – and must have met many Britons in the Caffè degli Inglesi, which stood in the square. Among them – from accounts of meetings, where his presence is mentioned – were George Romney, the painter, and Frederick Hervey, the enormously wealthy Bishop of Derry (later the Earl of Bristol) whose patronage every aspiring English artist or architect hoped to acquire. There was also James Byres, an architect and successful tourist-guide, who escorted many English gentlemen around Rome and southern Italy – the most famous being Edward Gibbon. Byres knew most people who mattered and, if he had befriended Harrison, the latter would have thought himself a fortunate man.

The early 1770s were a good time for an aspiring architect to be in Rome, a time of considerable ferment in ideas about art and Classical architecture. Harrison must have taken part in discussions within the Academy of St Luke – and between its students and those of the French Royal Academy, for some of his later work suggests knowledge of contemporary French designers, who prided themselves on the austere elegance and understated grandeur of their work. He cannot either have been unaware of the controversy about the origins of Roman architecture, which was then splitting the academic world in Italy, as it was in Britain.

Three centuries before, at the time of the Renaissance, Italian architects had introduced the idea of using 'antique '– that is, Roman – motifs in the design and decoration of modern buildings. Educated men and women in Georgian Britain, who believed that they were, so to speak, the heirs of

[Figure 1]
Rome: The Arch of Septimius Severus and the church of SS Luca e Martina, 1759 by Piranesi.

Rome, considered that the best source for contemporary design was therefore the architecture of the ancient Romans, and that the best 'authority' to justify any modern design was a known Classical model. However, by the middle of the eighteenth century it was recognised that the work of most architects since the Renaissance had not in fact been authentically Roman. Moreover, scholars were becoming aware that the Roman world had been bigger than they thought. By 1750 Roman buildings had been discovered not merely in Italy – under volcanic ash, as at Pompeii and Herculaneum – but also in North Africa and the Middle East, areas hitherto cut off from Western Europe, because they were part of the Ottoman Empire. Also, and more importantly, scholars came to realise that Roman ways of building had changed over time. The search for sure foundations for contemporary design in the 'antique manner'[*] led not unnaturally to the belief that an older source was 'better' – less 'corrupted' – than a newer source; however, the problem was that the number of Classical models was rising to the point, where few people could state with confidence what were 'authoritative' sources for contemporary work.

Coupled with these somewhat unnerving discoveries was a growing awareness of the architecture of Greece, then too part of the Ottoman Empire. Everyone knew that the 'golden age' of Greece had preceded the rise of Rome, but the corollary of this – that Athens was a better source than Rome for contemporary design – was not so easy to accept. While little was known of Greek architecture, this was a matter of little consequence. However, once the plans and façades of some of the buildings of Athens were published – the Frenchman, Julien David-Leroy had got there first in 1758, but was followed in 1762 by James Stuart and Nicholas Revett with their *Antiquities of Athens* – a long-running and sometimes acrimonious controversy began. Some people in England were pleased to adopt some of the new decorative motifs, which they found in Stuart's and Revett's book, though most established architects and their clients found Greek motifs interesting but inelegant. They were prepared to accept that Roman architecture was derived from Greek, but believed that the Romans had refined what they had found, and that their buildings still provided better models for contemporary designs.

In Italy this controversy about the superiority of Greek motifs was inflamed by the 'discovery' of three temples in the ruined town of Paestum, about 50 miles south of Naples. These had been known for centuries by sailors as landmarks, but had stood, unregarded in an area of malarial fenland, until the 1750s. We know now that these splendid temples were the work of Greek architects, but many Italians – out of a sort of national pride – could not accept this and preferred to believe that

---

[*] 'In the antique manner' was a vague phrase meaning using motifs believed to have been used in Classical times; for the same idea we now use the equally vague term 'neo-classical'.

they were the work of the Etruscans, the masters of Italy before the Romans, and that the architecture of Greece had therefore been derived from them.

The main apologist for the Greeks was the German archaeologist and art-historian, Johann Winckelmann, who believed that the only way forward for modern artists (and architects) was to imitate the Greeks. The most renowned of his Italian opponents was Giovanni Battista Piranesi (1720–78), a Venetian architect, who spent most of his life in Rome, where Harrison almost certainly met him. He was, and is, much more famous for his dramatic engravings of massive Roman ruins and of streets and squares in the contemporary City. However, although he had long praised the magnificence of Roman architecture and derided the claim that it was derived from the Greek, he decided to visit Paestum in 1778, despite serious illness. He was overwhelmed by the austere grandeur of the half-ruined temples and the expressive power of their sturdy Doric columns[*] – as his last engravings show. These were not published until after Harrison had left Italy, but I surmise that in later years Harrison remembered and reflected on Piranesi's reluctant but growing enthusiasm.

Harrison was not content just to study in Rome. In 1770, a year after his arrival, he – in Colvin's words – 'submitted to Pope Clement XIV a design for converting the Cortile del Belvedere in the Vatican into a museum, which was favourably received but not in the end adopted.'[5] (This courtyard is now known as the Cortile Ottagono and stands within the Palazetto del Belvedere.) No drawing of Harrison's design survives, but Canon Blomfield[†], who delivered the first paper on Harrison – it was reprinted in *The Builder* of 21 March 1863 – described the scheme as 'surrounding the

---

[*] Classical columns have been grouped – since the time of the Romans – into three 'orders' (or styles) according to the details of their columns and entablatures (the beams or lintels, which the columns support). Doric columns are fairly squat (their height is by convention seven times their diameter), their capitals are simple in shape, and their entablatures are recognisable by the triglyphs (grooved blocks representing beam-ends) in the frieze. (A simpler, and cheaper, version of the Doric without the triglyphs is called the Tuscan order.) The columns of the Ionic order are more slender (eight times as high as their diameter) and their capitals have volutes (which look rather like ringlets). Corinthian columns are more slender again and their capitals are ornately decorated with acanthus leaves. The Doric order was the earliest to be used in ancient Greece and was therefore regarded by some scholars in the later eighteenth century, despite its relative inelegance – it was shorter than in the Roman form and stood without a base on the ground – as the purest and most authentic of all the orders.

[†] Rev. George Blomfield, a canon of Chester Cathedral, was the younger brother of the Bishop of Chester, who was present when the first stone of the Grosvenor Bridge there was laid in 1827 (see page 125). He was also the uncle of the Victorian architect, Sir Arthur Blomfield. His paper was stimulated by a description of the Grosvenor Bridge by an architectural historian, who praised the engineer, Jesse Hartley, but did not mention Harrison.

interior of the court with a rich cloister or arcade 100 feet long each way and covering the inclosed space, about 54 feet square, with a noble circular dome'. Harrison's dome was compared at the time by an Italian critic, Francesco Milizia, to the one in the Pantheon – the best preserved of any Roman building in Rome, because it had been converted for use as a church in 609. It is not clear what Milizia meant by this comparison – whether he had in mind the hemi-spherical shape and coffering of the interior, or the shallow profile of the exterior; or, of course, all of them. Whatever be the case, Harrison certainly used features of the Pantheon's stupendous dome in his designs from the very beginning of his career.

Harrison's scheme for the Cortile was regarded as unrealistic, as well as being the work of a young foreigner, but it later brought him to the notice of the Pope, who was the patron of the Academy of St Luke, and this had fortunate consequences for him. In 1773 he competed in the Academy's biennial competition for an architectural prize, which also guaranteed membership of the Academy. The brief was to create an impressive and symmetrical design to improve the appearance of the Piazza del Popolo in Rome, which lies immediately inside the northern gate of the old City.

The Piazza, from which three straight streets lead to various parts of the centre, was hardly an imposing entrance to the City of Rome in 1773. The inner façade of the Porta del Popolo had, to be sure, been brought up-to-date in 1665 with paired columns and a curved pediment by Bernini. A few years later another architect had improved the grandeur of the Piazza's southern side by placing between the three streets two churches with tall domes and imposing porticos – their paired Corinthian columns are a modification by Bernini. However, between the Gate and the churches there was little more than a roughly triangular space, containing an Egyptian obelisk; it was flanked on the east by the plain façade of an Augustinian priory church and a garden wall, and on the west by some nondescript buildings.

Harrison did not win the prize. His beautifully drawn design, which was almost certainly the one which he exhibited at the Royal Academy in London in 1777 and which is now in the Cheshire Record Office,[6] is very different from the designs of the Italian architects who won the first and second prizes. It is not difficult to see why they did so. Their designs reflect the tall domes of the two existing churches and are liberally furnished with the then fashionable colonnades. Harrison's design, on the other hand, proposes a monumental ensemble for each of the two sides of the triangle. [Figure 2] In the centre is a church (one of them for the Augustinians) with a tall pedimented portico of six Ionic columns – more 'correctly' Roman than Bernini's paired columns. The church is set between and behind a pair of small square chapels, which have shallow, Pantheon-like domes, and is linked to them by concave quadrant walls. These are faced by Doric half-columns with a full entablature. The chapel façades to the Piazza also have

this Doric colonnade, but with widely spaced columns and with a lower arch between the two centre columns – a motif, which was meant to recall a Roman triumphal arch. The triglyph frieze continues further on either side above the long outer wings. The narrow north side of the Piazza is totally re-cast as a 17-bay screen wall, decorated by Doric half-columns and frieze, and Bernini's gate is replaced by a triumphal arch with four pairs of projecting Doric columns.

There is a notable consistency to this design, in the use of the Doric order everywhere except in front of the churches; and these dominant churches, with their simple, tall, pedimented porticoes would have formed an interesting contrast with Bernini's more sculptural façades on the churches on the south side. But that will have been part of the problem for Harrison, as he sought to defend his proposals. Piranesi and James Byres are said to have approved of Harrison's scheme, and it would appear that it did receive some public praise. The problem for Harrison was that his design used motifs like Pantheon domes, Roman temple porticos and triumphal arches, which were derived from current archaeological research, for a square whose main elements came from the hand of one of Italy's most famous architects.

On the day following the announcement of the results Harrison petitioned the Pope to allow his drawings to be exhibited in the Capitol along with those of the two prize-winners – the normal procedure in the case of disputes. This was done. The Pope asked the President of the

CR 73/20

[Figure 2]
Extract from
Harrison's
competition design
for the Piazza del
Popolo in Rome,
1773. Reproduced
by permission of
Cheshire and
Chester Archives
and Local Studies.

Academy for a report, but this cleared the Academy of the charge of bias. Harrison immediately petitioned the Pope again, claiming that his scheme had been acclaimed by the public. Within three weeks he was informed that, though he would not win a prize, he had been created an *accademico di merito* – not a full member, but one elected on the recommendation of a member. He was in good company: the Academy records show that other British architects like Robert Mylne and George Dance had been similarly honoured.

We do not know by which route Harrison returned to England three years later, but in the Cheshire Record Office there is a plan in his hand of the Maison Carrée in Nîmes, and his later use of motifs drawn from recent buildings in Paris, like Jacques Gondoin's Ecole de chirurgie and Jean Perronet's Pont de Neuilly, suggests that he passed through there as well. Indeed, the considered – rather than just intuitive – understanding of the structures of bridges and of the forces within them, which he was to show in his designs for Skerton Bridge in Lancaster, make it highly probable that he had been in contact with the engineers of Perronet's renowned Ecole des ponts et chaussées; but there is no proof.

When he returned to England in 1776, Harrison was 32 and still had to find a client willing to employ a talented young man with no track record. In the spring of 1777 he must have been living in London, when he exhibited two of his drawings for the Piazza del Popolo at the Royal Academy. This was the normal procedure for an architect, who wanted to make a name for himself, since the annual exhibition of the Academy attracted about 20,000 visitors. At about the same time he also made designs – speculatively – for a monumental bridge over the Thames on the site later used by Waterloo Bridge, and then for a road along the Thames from Westminster Bridge past the new Adelphi buildings, and the building site of the new Somerset House, to the recently completed Blackfriars Bridge. Nothing, however, came of these schemes, or of the contacts, which he had made at Rome. He will doubtless have seen many fine new buildings in London, like Wyatt's Pantheon – so called because of its dome-like central space – and Dance's Newgate Prison, but it was not a good time to try to start a career there. War had broken out with the American colonists, and building work virtually stopped: Bedford Square was begun in 1776, but took seven years to complete. Harrison had to return to Richmond in 1778. What he did next is not yet known. He sent drawings to the Royal Academy exhibitions in 1779 and 1780, but again without success.

Designing visionary buildings might bring an architect into the public eye, but success normally depended on more than large-scale fantasies. Architects who wanted to practise as such, rather than be employed as draftsmen, had – then as now – to design buildings, which their clients liked and which could be built at an affordable price and within the limitations of the technologies of the day. (Harrison was fortunate, since cast iron, as well as wrought iron, had been available to builders for a generation, and quarrying and lifting techniques had made it possible to produce and handle the large stones, which he wanted to use for his more monumental works.) Most importantly, of course, new buildings had to be convenient to use – unless they were built solely to display a client's wealth or patriotism – but even monumental buildings have to withstand the weather and the normal wear and tear of use.

CHAPTER TWO

Harrison's First Known Work: Skerton Bridge, Lancaster, 1782–87

Harrison's later work proved that he could design buildings, which would work well and look well, but he had to find the opportunity to show this. After his return from London, he must have hoped for some help from Sir Lawrence Dundas. However, the leading Yorkshire architect, John Carr, had designed some family rooms and a stable block at Aske Hall about ten years before, and Dundas did not want anything more in a house which was no longer important to him. Harrison does not appear to have designed anything at Richmond; there are some attractive mid-Georgian houses in the town, but nothing which could not have been designed by a competent building craftsman. He had to look further afield.

He presumably read as widely as he could, in the days before technical magazines could be found in public libraries, and presumably kept his eyes and ears open for what had been recently done in Yorkshire. In the 1760s and '70s Robert Adam had made significant alterations to the major country houses, Newby Hall and Nostell Priory, and John Carr had worked on a dozen others, like Harewood and Constable Burton, as well as designing a few bridges. Is it possible that Harrison acted as a clerk of works on one of these sites? This was then a normal way for a young man to launch a professional career as an architect. He appears to have known the façades and plans of a number of houses by Adam and Carr, and Carr certainly knew of Harrison later and thought well of his work. It is impossible to believe that his design work in the 1780s and afterwards could have been technically so competent, unless he had had serious practical involvement in the actual building of a major house, but, as yet, we do not know. It is also possible – in view of his later success as a designer of prisons, and of the description of him in the minutes of the Lancashire Quarter Sessions in October 1786 as a 'professed prison architect' – that he entered, and did well in, the competition in 1782 for the design of the planned National Penitentiary in London. However, for the moment, this can be nothing but pure speculation.

It must, therefore, have been with relief and elation that he received the news in December 1782, that he had won the first prize of 20 guineas in the competition, organised by the Lancashire County authorities, to design and build a new bridge over the Lune from Skerton to Lancaster. The second prize was won by Samuel Weston, a canal surveyor and contractor from Chester,[1] while the winner of the third prize, John Gott of Leeds, was the engineer of the Aire and Calder Navigation and Surveyor of Bridges for the West Riding.[2]

Designing and building a bridge involves many more skills than building a house. A bridge is an arched structure, so one has to understand the sideways thrust within arches and know how to build them and their abutments properly. One needs also to know how to build foundations under the water to carry piers, which will be strong enough to withstand the thrust of the arches, but not so broad that they obstruct the flow of water. The fact that Harrison beat Gott and Weston must prove that he was well versed in traditional bridge-building techniques. The records also suggest that he was *au fait* with the work of Jean Perronet.

The competition came about in 1782, because there was no such man in Lancashire as a professional County Surveyor and Bridgemaster, responsible for the maintenance of existing bridges in the County and the building of new ones. John Gott had been the Surveyor of Bridges for the West Riding since 1777, and John Carr had held a similar post in the North Riding since 1772. But Lancashire, within its traditional boundaries, was large and long and narrow – not a shape to encourage centralisation; it did not appoint one County Bridgemaster until 1900. Instead, most of the six 'Hundreds', into which the County was then divided for administrative convenience, had a man called the Bridgemaster. However, he was only a gentleman amateur (experienced, but not professionally trained) who organised the repair of failing bridges, or the building of simple new ones, by builders known to be competent. In more difficult cases, as at Lancaster, the County's magistrates or Justices of the Peace (the then equivalent of the County Council) organised competitions, by advertising in local newspapers and inviting 'artificers and workmen' to tender designs for a new bridge with estimates of the cost.

Harrison arrived at a timely moment in Lancaster. Something of a lull had followed the boom in public buildings in the 1750s and 60s – probably because the port was not developing as fast as hoped. Henry Sephton, from Liverpool, had completed the tower of St Mary's Church (now the Priory) in 1755, and in the same year St John's Chapel had been finished. In 1759 the trustees of Penny's Hospital had asked someone – probably Richard Gillow – to design the Assembly Room next door. In 1764 Gillow's elegant Customs House (now the Maritime Museum) had been completed – with its impressive, 16-foot monolithic Ionic columns – on the new St George's Quay.

By 1782, however, Sephton was dead, and Gillow was concentrating on furniture. There was, however, Edward Batty, who is described as an architect on his memorial tablet outside St John's Church. In 1783 he was asked by John Dalton, of Thurnham Hall, to lay out Dalton Square and the surrounding streets within his Friarage estate, but he cannot have been regarded as an architect, competent to design a major building project, since he had not been asked in 1781 to design the Town Hall in Lancaster (now the City Museum). The design was in fact produced by a retired military engineer, Major Thomas Jarratt.

Skerton Bridge [Figure 3] was intended to replace Lancaster's medieval bridge, which crossed the river between the end of Bridge Lane and what is now Lune Street in Skerton. The old bridge had for some time been showing signs of distress and was 'indicted' by the Grand Jury of County magistrates during the Quarter Sessions in January 1782. An application was then made to Parliament for an Act, which would allow the building of a new bridge at a more convenient site. This was supported by a petition from the townspeople and was passed in June 1782. The new bridge was also intended to provide a grander entrance to the town, and Cable Street was laid out at the Borough's expense over the waste ground of the Green Ayre, in the hope of encouraging the development of housing along the river. (The Green Ayre was laid out in building plots by Batty in 1783, but the hopes of high-class development were never fulfilled.)

Harrison won the competition, but the County's committee wanted some amendments. The committee was chaired by Richard Threlfall, the

[Figure 3]
Lancaster: Skerton
Bridge, *c.*2000.

Bridgemaster of the Amounderness Hundred, who had recently supervised the building of County bridges over the Ribble near Ribchester in 1774–5 and at Walton-le-Dale in 1779–81. Harrison met Threlfall, and they agreed that the overall width of the bridge structure should be reduced by two feet, that the piers should be one foot taller, and that the foundations should be sunk one foot lower below the low water level. Harrison was appointed as supervisor of the works, and contractors were sought for the project, which had been costed at £10,400.

The approved contractors were a team under the leadership of Benjamin Muschamp, a mason from Otley in Yorkshire. Four other masons in his team also shared the same surname and were therefore probably related. (We do not know how these men were found, but Harrison probably suggested them.) The masons were joined by two carpenters from Otley, whose work would be essential for the placing of the foundations and the building – and, later, the removal – of the timber centring, which was necessary to support the stone arches, while the lime mortar slowly dried.

The contract, known as the *Articles for building Lancaster bridge*,[3] was signed and sealed on 21 February 1783. It has an appended drawing, which shows the plan and elevation of the bridge. Harrison had to provide working drawings – none have survived – and the contractors were responsible for finding the necessary stone, timber, lime and sand, and would be responsible for any repairs and maintenance necessary during the first seven years after completion. The Borough Corporation agreed that the contractors might obtain sandstone from any of the quarries on the waste ground, belonging to it – basically, those in what is now Williamson Park.[4]

The *Articles* specify that the masonry piers and abutments of the bridge would be built on foundations twelve feet deep, formed of oak or 'foreign firr' piles, ten inches square and no more than 18 inches apart. The outer piles would be grooved so that sheeting piles could be driven down between them to create a solid perimeter, which would act as a coffer dam – a more or less water-tight wall – within which the masonry piers could be built. Between the heads of the piles a sort of concrete, made of rubble, gravel, lime and sand, would be rammed, and then six-inch planks of Baltic timber would be spiked to the heads of the piles to form a grille, on which the first courses of the masonry of the piers would be laid. The stones, of which the piers were to be built, would be 15 inches deep and 30 inches long. The 'binders', which were laid at right angles to the side walls of the piers, would be at least six feet long, so that they stretched more than half-way across each pier, which was 11 feet wide. The gaps between the main stones would be built up solid with dressed stones – not rubble – 15 inches deep, and each course would be laid and pointed in a good strong lime mortar. The voussoirs – the wedge-shaped stones which form the actual arches – would be 30 inches tall at the crown of the arch and three feet at its springing, and the spandrels, that is the visible walls above the arches, would be built of stones 15 inches thick and backed by solid masonry. All stones would have to be cut accurately, so that only the minimum of mortar need be used.

It was a good specification. A well designed and well built stone bridge with good abutments, provided that it is well maintained, will last 'for ever', and an examination in 1995 ascertained that Skerton Bridge is strong enough, as built, to carry vehicles weighing 40 tons – ten times the weight (at, probably, ten times the speed) of the heaviest vehicles in 1783. We can, moreover, be confident that what was planned was built, since the engineer, John Rennie (who later became a friend of Harrison) visited the site in March 1784 and noted the oak piles and the fact that the piers were being built within coffer dams.

Nothing remains in the records of the actual brief for the competition for Skerton Bridge. However, an eight-page hand-written document in the Lancashire County Record Office, called *References to different designs for a Bridge over the River Loyne at Lancaster by Thomas Harrison*,[5] allows one to make inferences about the major concerns of the County's JPs. The *References* are in effect a series of explanatory notes by Harrison on the chosen design, a justification of the innovative features of the bridge. They make the implied assertion that he had substantial experience, and that he was aware not only of what had recently been built in Britain, but also of some Continental examples. They also make clear that he had made alternative designs – which suggests that he was anxious to show his versatility.

Harrison described his scheme as 'consisting of five elliptical arches, each 60 Feet wide, making 300 Feet Water Way, which may be increased 30 or 40 Feet, if thought necessary'. The width of his proposed new bridge would be 'nearly 37 feet, which after allowing for the Parapets, affords 24 Feet for the Carriage Way and 5 Feet on each Side for the Foot Paths'. *The Cumberland Pacquet* of 31 October 1787 stated that each arch spanned 68 feet and rose 19 feet 6 inches, which proves that Harrison's suggestion of an increased 'water way' was accepted. It also gave the total length of the bridge as 216 yards.

Wide arches would have been welcome to the Lancashire JPs, who cannot have forgotten that in 1771 the County bridge near Ribchester had been destroyed, when trees, carried down by floodwater, had blocked the arches and thus dammed the river, until the pressure of the water pushed the arches and piers away. However, wide spans must also have worried them, because Harrison was at pains to reassure them. 'These Arches may be thought large, but the Arches of the fine new Bridge built over the Seine near Paris, are 130 Feet Diameter, Semi-ellipses and very low'.[*] Harrison was also keen to stress the advantages of semi-elliptical arches – 'by rising the quickest at

---

[*] This bridge was the (now demolished) Pont de Neuilly, designed by Jean Perronet, which was opened in 1772.

the Springing [they] afford the most Water Way and [are] therefore the most proper for low Arches'. (There was actually nothing new about semi-elliptical arches; Robert Mylne had used them for his Blackfriars Bridge in London, designed in 1760.)

Harrison was eager to show that he understood – as well as anyone did then, before it was possible to measure them accurately – the forces which act sideways in an arched structure. He explained how, to give the masonry 'greater Strength, the Joints of the Masonry on the Sides of the Arches are continued in a line with the Joints of the Pens or Archstones'. [Figure 4] These archstones [= voussoirs] are in fact almost all so cut as to provide collectively a decorative archband and also to interlock individually with the stones of the spandrel walls – an expensive but doubly elegant detail, seen on all of Harrison's earlier bridges which are built of easily worked stone. This interlocking of the voussoirs and the stones of the spandrels had been practised by the Romans and probably gives a little help to prevent an arch bursting at its haunches. Such an intuitive understanding was in fact part of good traditional practice, but to make it visually explicit in this way – by hinting that the voussoirs transmit the forces within an arch – suggests that Harrison was, more than most English architects of his time, interested in structures as well as aesthetics.

The first stone of Skerton Bridge was laid in June 1783 by John Fenton-

[Figure 4] Lancaster: Skerton Bridge – detail showing how the voussoirs interlock with the stones in the spandrel walls, *c.*2000.

[Figure 5]
John Landseer's
engraving of
Skerton Bridge,
1791.

Cawthorne, the Recorder of Lancaster, in the presence of the Council,[6] and the work was finished in September 1787, at a cost of £14,000.[7] It is perhaps the most beautiful bridge in Lancashire with its five semi-elliptical arches, which carry the road deck on a flat line, rather than rising to the centre in the traditional way. [Figure 5] It is often said to be the first example of this feature in England; this may be true, though John Smeaton had done the same at Coldstream in Scotland in 1763, and Harrison does no more than refer to it obliquely in the *References*.

The cutwaters are semi-circular in plan and rusticated to form (as Palladian taste demanded) a contrasting basement to the ashlar of the rest of the structure. They are each surmounted by a solidly built niche, which passes right through the structure and is capped by a pediment carried on Tuscan columns, to form what is called an aedicule. These aedicules help to stress the vertical, and thus counter the horizontal emphasis, given to the bridge by its well-defined cornice and balustrade. Harrison described them in the *References* as 'giving an Air of Lightness to the Bridge; also lessening the Weight on the Peirs [*sic*].' He continued – in what is a good example of the justification of a contemporary design by reference to a Roman precedent, mentioned on page 9 – 'Openings of this Kind are to seen in the Senatorial Bridge in Rome'.[*]

Just after its completion, Skerton Bridge was described in *The*

___

[*] This is the bridge, now called the Ponte Fabricio, which was built in 61 BC; the primary purpose of the arches there was probably to relieve the pressure of floodwater in the Tiber, and this may have been a consideration at Lancaster too.

Cumberland Paquet on 31 October 1787 as 'worthy of the observation of travellers…the chief ornament of the place'. It was soon praised in a traveller's diary of 1792 as ' a very handsome bridge of five arches' leading to 'a very good, handsome wide avenue'.[8] By then the artist, Joseph Farington, had made an attractive, though slightly inaccurate, watercolour drawing of the bridge in front of the Castle and the Priory Church on their hill.[9] This was the basis of the engraving, made by John Landseer in 1791, which has since become the best-known image of Lancaster.

CHAPTER THREE

Other Early Bridges, 1788–93

Skerton Bridge was the springboard for Harrison's later career. However, before describing his major projects at Lancaster and Chester Castles, it is appropriate to look briefly at his work on other bridges, which arose from Skerton Bridge.

His success in Lancaster meant that he was soon asked to design bridges elsewhere. The first was **St Mary's Bridge** in **Derby**, which was designed in 1788 and still stands at the point from which roads run towards Chesterfield and Nottingham. The River Derwent is about 50 yards wide there. Harrison's bridge replaced a medieval structure which had become too narrow to cope with carriages and wagons and was deemed to be dangerous.

Some of the minutes of Derby Borough's Bridge Committee[1] still survive and show that in January 1787 a 'Mr Wyatt of Burton' was invited to produce a plan. At the same time John Carr of York was asked to recommend 'five or six proper persons' to design a new bridge. He gave the names of three men – John Gott from Leeds, William Jessop, a well-respected canal engineer from Newark, and William Bellwood, a competent architect in York – plus that of Harrison. (From this we can infer that Carr, who described Harrison as an architect from York, had seen something of his work and been impressed by it.) The Committee wrote to Jessop and Harrison in March and preferred the latter's scheme. The foundation stone was laid in November 1789, and work was complete in 1793, although the date 1794 is carved on a pier.

The bridge is faced with sandstone ashlar and is clearly a smaller version of Skerton Bridge [Figure 6]. It has the same flat road deck and rusticated cutwaters, but only three semi-elliptical arches and shallow niches in the piers. Each arch has a span of 48 feet and, as at Skerton Bridge, the voussoirs are cut both to provide an archband and to interlock with the stones of the spandrels.

Harrison designed a second bridge in Derbyshire – the *Harrington Bridge* at *Sawley*, of which there are very slight remains. It was built between April 1789 and September 1790 to replace a ferry over the River Trent and to carry a road from Nottingham to Ashby de la Zouch. Since the clerk to the trustees, who organised the building of the bridge, was a Bryan Grey from Lancaster, who appears to have been a lawyer with canal interests, it may well be he who suggested Harrison's name.

[Figure 6]
Derby: St Mary's
Bridge, 2004.

The main channel of the river is some 50 yards wide and is now spanned by a steel girder bridge. However, its abutments with three courses of rusticated sandstone masonry correspond to those shown in a drawing, 'produced by Mr Harrison' and now in the Derbyshire County Record Office.[2] The bridge rose slightly to the centre on three arches. The specification for the actual structure of the bridge is very similar to that for Skerton Bridge.

Nearer home Harrison won a competition in 1791, with a prize of ten guineas, to design a new **Stramongate Bridge**, in **Kendal.** The medieval bridge carried the main road to Scotland over the River Kent, and its structure had been giving concern for decades.[3] Harrison's design was for a bridge, 30 feet wide between the parapets, with three semi-elliptical arches, the central one having a span of 50 feet and the side ones a span of 45 feet. No drawing now survives.

An advertisement was then placed in September 1791 in three regional newspapers – *Gore's Liverpool General Advertiser, The Leeds Intelligencer* and *The Cumberland Paquet* – asking contractors to give a price for building the bridge 'after a design of Mr Harrison's of Lancaster'. A contract was signed by William Holme and Francis Webster of Kendal in 1793. However, when the work of demolishing the old bridge was begun, it was found that the core of one of the piers was 'indestructible'. Harrison had therefore to produce another plan to accommodate this pier, for which he was paid a further ten guineas.[4] Work on the revised scheme began in 1794 – the date is visible over a cutwater on the upstream side. Harrison was not paid for his drawings until January 1796, with a further £10 for his attendance (that is, supervision of the work) in October 1797.

The bridge, as built, has *four segmental* arches. Its voussoirs, the band at road level and the parapet are fairly smooth-faced, but the rest of the masonry is more roughly dressed.[*] The piers are decorated by shallow, round-headed niches. The arches have an archband, but the voussoirs do not interlock with the stones of the spandrels. The three western arches are similar in profile and originally carried a level road surface, but the eastern arch has a narrower span and is lop-sided; it is all somewhat ungainly.

Harrison was also employed in Lancashire. Ockrim reports that in 1792 he was asked by the JPs to make copies of the Bridge Books for the Lonsdale Hundred.[5] These volumes were illustrated with plans and elevations of each bridge and gave such information as the width of the waterway and the length of the road over the bridge for which the JPs were responsible. It is not clear that Harrison accepted this request, since a County-wide set of Bridge Books was prepared in 1805 (and is now in the Lancashire County Record Office).[6] Ockrim adds that Harrison was later asked to report on 70 bridges north of Morecambe Bay, but it is not clear from the records that he obliged.

Ockrim further reports that in July 1793 he was asked to use his professional skills and oversee the rebuilding of three bridges in the Lonsdale Hundred.[7] *Cocker Bridge* has been replaced by a pair of sluice-gates, but Harrison probably had a hand in the other two, which appear in the Bridge Book of 1805. **Mill House Bridge** is no more than a culvert, measuring about six feet high by four feet wide, with a semi-circular arch and an inverted arch under the stream itself, all faced with hammer-dressed sandstone. **Denny Beck Bridge** carries the Lancaster-Richmond turnpike (now the A683) across an incised valley, perhaps 20 feet deep; the older part of the present bridge has abutments about 10 feet tall and a semi-circular arch with a span of about 20 feet. Apart from the plain parapets all the facing stonework is rusticated. Both of these bridges might date from 1793, but they have no architectural pretensions and could have been designed and built by any competent contractor, under Harrison's supervision or not.

While engaged in the research for this book, I came across an attractive drawing among the Harrison papers in the Cheshire Record Office.[8] [Figure 7] In the catalogue it is called simply a 'bridge of five bays', but it is clearly a bridge near Lancaster, since through its arches one can see what can only be Skerton Bridge with the Castle and Priory Church on their hill behind it. There is no scale on the drawing, but the bridge's arches have a span of some 40 feet and spring from piers, which are about 20 feet tall. The voussoirs interlock with the spandrels, and every stone is rusticated, even in the undersides of the arches. The parapet is simply arcaded. This bridge

---

[*] Before the introduction of water-powered saws *c.*1800 the local limestone was almost impossible to work to a smooth and accurate finish.

[Figure 7]
Harrison's design
for the canal
aqueduct over the
Lune at Lancaster,
*c.*1795. Reproduced
by permission of
Cheshire and
Chester Archives
and Local Studies.

was clearly meant to run flat from bank to bank across the river upstream
of Skerton Bridge and must have been intended to carry the Lancaster Canal
over the Lune. Since, however, there is no mention in the Lancaster Canal
archives of a competition for the design of the Lune aqueduct, this must
be a speculative design by Harrison. It is a fine utilitarian structure, but no
rival to the present monumental aqueduct, which was built by Alexander
Stevens to the designs of John Rennie.

CHAPTER FOUR

Other Works in Lancaster, 1782–95

Harrison's professional career had begun in Lancaster in 1782 with the major project of Skerton Bridge and continued there until 1798 with the even larger scheme at the Castle. Between those dates he was also designing other works, which, for want of a better word, one has to call minor – though the word does not do justice to the now demolished Springfield Hall.

When Harrison arrived in Lancaster, a new Town Hall (now the **City Museum**) was being built on the Market Square to the designs of Major Jarratt. [Figure 8] With its six Roman Doric half-columns, rising through both storeys on the main façade, and its pedimented portico and triglyph entablature, carried on four similarly tall Doric columns – such columns, rising to the height of two storeys, are called giant columns – it has a simple grandeur, which may well have appealed to a man who had known Piranesi. However, the Borough Council decided not to build the cupola which Jarratt had designed to stand above the pediment. Consequently, Harrison, who had just won the Skerton Bridge competition and was described as an architect from Richmond in Yorkshire, was asked to design the present **clock tower** in December 1782 – before work began on Skerton Bridge.

It is an attractive work, with an octagonal base housing the clock and supporting a rotunda with eight tall Ionic columns around the bell-turret; above this is a low drum, decorated with the then fashionable garlands and capped by a little dome. The whole piece nicely balances solidity, to match the lower parts of the building, with some grace in the upper parts. The Council was so pleased that in December 1783 it offered Harrison the Freedom of the Corporation as thanks for his 'Attention and Assistance'.

Perhaps on the strength of this work, Harrison was asked in 1783 to add a **tower and spire at St John's Chapel**. [Figure 9] The attribution to 'the ingenious Mr Harrison' was made in *The Cumberland Pacquet* of 22 April 1783.[1] This work was doubtless undertaken to give a greater consequence to the chapel, which was often used by the Borough Corporation, and was paid for from the estate of Thomas Bowes, a merchant and member of the Corporation, who had worshipped there before his death in 1783.

[Figure 8]
Lancaster: Town
Hall, showing
Harrison's clock
tower, 1829.

[Figure 9]
Lancaster:
St John's Church,
showing Harrison's
tower and spire,
c.1930. Reproduced
by courtesy of
Lancaster City
Museums.

The tower is faced with ashlar and is a sensitive piece of work, relating well to the existing church and well proportioned in its own right. The west door and the tops of the ground-floor windows of the tower match those of the church; its three stages are separated by cornices, but the middle cornice – at the height of the church roof – is more pronounced and, in its visual effect, separates the tower from the spire. The lower stage of the spire contains a wide belfry opening on each face, within a Tuscan aedicule. Above this is a robust rotunda with eight Doric half-columns, carrying a triglyph frieze and a low drum, decorated with garlands, from which rises a spire with eight concave sides.

The rotundas at both the Old Town Hall and St John's Chapel were loosely based on a famous Classical monument in Athens, now called the Choragic Monument of Lysicrates. It had been built in 334 BC, incorporated into a much later building and then 'discovered' in the 1750s, after which it was illustrated in Stuart and Revett's *Antiquities*. It consists basically of a cylinder, about 20 feet high and 6 feet in diameter, surrounded by six fluted, Corinthian half-columns. It stands on a square base and is capped by a shallow dome.[*] Stuart designed a copy of the monument for the park at Shugborough in Staffordshire, where it was completed in 1771. Harrison seems to have been the first architect, anywhere, to use it as an inspiration for a new design, rather than to copy it exactly – which is one measure of his significance in the history of English architecture.

Harrison's next work in Lancaster was to embank the Green Ayre and design the so-called **Bridge Houses** to mark the entrance to the town. [Figure 10] The commission was given, not by the County, but by the Borough, which paid him 15 guineas in 1790 for making the plans and 'overlooking' the building work.[2] The central house was built in 1786 for use as a toll-house, the others for renting out in 1787. Their individual plans are typical of most middle-sized houses in Lancaster, but the façade of the group follows the Palladian format for a building of consequence, that is a central block flanked by lower wings and pavilions. The principal facades are faced with ashlar. The central hip-roofed pavilion has two storeys and three bays, emphasised by pairs of Greek Ionic[†] half-columns on the tall first floor. The base of these columns continues to both sides as a moulded

---

[*] The dome originally carried a bronze tripod won by the poet, Lysicrates, in a competition to write and stage a chorus, performed as part of the ceremonies in honour of the god, Dyonisus.

[†] As distinct from its Roman form, which was normally used until about 1780 and can be seen in the clock tower of the City Museum in Lancaster, the capital of the Greek Ionic order, which only became known after the publication of pictures of it in the 1760s, has volutes which are in the plane of the wall above them, and not set to project at 45 degrees. This was Harrison's first use of the motif, but he used it in every later building, and so the word 'Ionic' will from now on be used to mean 'Greek Ionic'.

band to cap the screen and then serves as a sill-band to the first-floor windows of the pedimented pavilions. This once elegant and imposing ensemble is now being refurbished after years of neglect, but is still disfigured by tall street-lamps and a hump-backed roadway.

[Figure 10]
Lancaster: The
Bridge Houses,
c.1990.

* * *

The contract for Skerton Bridge and the regular income, which it ensured, encouraged Harrison to make his home in Lancaster. The usual practice by the 1780s in England was that, once a design and cost estimate had been approved, an architect was given an advance on the normally accepted five per cent fee for design and supervision; it was thereafter his responsibility – not the client's – to find the materials and the craftsmen to carry out the work, and to claim payment of the rest as appropriate.[3]

The JPs' records show that Harrison was living in Lancaster in 1786,[4] and he is thought to have lived and worked in one of the houses in Chapel Street opposite St John's. It is likely that he moved to Lancaster earlier than 1786, since in 1785 he married a local woman, Margaret Shackleton, in St Mary's Church. He was then 40 years old. They had in time five children, of whom two daughters were to survive him. Three children were certainly born in Lancaster – John in 1789, Eliza in 1791 and Anne in 1793.

It seems clear that, once he had achieved his ambition and was accepted as an architect, Harrison was unwilling to undertake any work which did not involve creative design. His apparent reluctance to make copies of the Lonsdale Hundred bridge books has already been mentioned. An earlier example comes from November 1790, when he was asked by the Borough to make a survey of the stone quarries on Lancaster Moor; the fact that in December 1792 someone else was asked to do the same job suggests that Harrison had declined. [5]

* * *

In addition to his public works Harrison is said to have designed St Anne's Church and a few houses for private clients in Lancaster. Greycourt on St Mary's Gate, the Reform Club on Great Saint John Street and the similar house on Water Street, plus Dacrelands in Skerton, have all been suggested. So too have the Gillison's Almshouses, which stood on Common Garden Street. All have, or had, attractive and even elegant façades, but there is no documentary evidence for Harrison's involvement. In my view, Greycourt (which shares some window details with Kennet House) and St Anne's Church (whose incumbent was related to the Keeper of the Castle) are possibly by Harrison. They were designed when he lived in Lancaster and have the austerity and good proportions common to much of his work, but the question of attribution to him must remain open.

There is slight evidence that he designed a house on the corner of Castle Hill and Meeting House Lane for the merchant, Thomas Rawlinson. A block plan, dated 14 December 1784, shows plans for steps and railings, but no more.[6] A wide-fronted house stood on the site in 1798 and can be seen in the background of figure 8. A photograph, taken before the building of the Storey Institute in 1887, shows a five-bay town house with a central pedimented porch, but there is nothing about its design which suggests that Harrison was more than possibly involved.

There was, however, another house in Lancaster, which was almost certainly designed by Harrison, and that was *Springfield Hall*, which, until it was demolished in 1962, stood on the site of what is now the Centenary Building of the Royal Lancaster Infirmary. It was a large suburban villa, rather than a town house, and was built for James Hargreaves, who owned a plantation in Jamaica and a sugar-house in St Leonardgate and was also a partner in Dilworth and Hargreaves' Bank. He died in 1804.[7]

There is no documentary evidence for Harrison's involvement at Springfield. Ockrim rejects the idea, and Colvin therefore does not mention it, but I attribute the house to Harrison with almost certainty on the grounds of stylistic similarities to works which are known to be by him. A mid-nineteenth-century illustration[8] shows a two-storey house with three wide bays under a hipped roof, with a curved porch on columns set between tripartite windows, and the 50-inch OS map of Lancaster, published in 1849, shows that its facade was about 60 feet wide. A postcard of *c*.1900 in

the Lancaster City Museum[9] shows even more. [Figure 11] The first-floor windows had typically Georgian 12-pane sashes – four panes high and three wide – like the slightly taller ones on the ground floor; the service wing ended in a little pedimented pavilion. The house was faced with large blocks of ashlar; the porch had monolithic Tuscan columns, and the tripartite windows on the ground floor had square mullions under a segmental relieving arch.[*] All these features are paralleled in Kennet House, which Harrison certainly designed in 1793, and most of them can be found in the house, Woodbank, near Stockport, which he almost certainly designed in 1812. Like every other house, known to have been designed by Harrison, Springfield Hall was well placed on its site to enjoy good views.

The *Victoria County History* gave the date of the house as '*c.* 1790',[10] and Hewitson[11] wrote 'about 1792', while Cross Fleury[12] stated that it had been 'erected about 1790–93.' Twycross[13] wrote in 1847 that the house was 'erected at the commencement of the present century'. None of the authors gives a source for his information, but, if the *VCH*, Hewitson and Cross Fleury are correct, I believe that Springfield was Harrison's earliest house and therefore the source of the design of the more sophisticated Kennet House, which was the basis of several of his later houses.

[Figure 11]
Lancaster;
Springfield Hall,
*c.*1900. Reproduced
by courtesy of
Lancaster City
Museums.

---

[*] Such windows had probably been first used by Samuel Wyatt, the elder brother of the more famous James, at Doddington Hall in Cheshire in 1777 and had quickly become fashionable.

There are no illustrations of the interior, but aerial photographs suggest that its plan was typical of a villa of that period, with an entrance hall leading to a top-lit stairhall and with reception rooms on the right, looking down over Morecambe Bay to the Lake District hills. Sixty years ago the staircase rose in a single flight to a half-landing, from which two flights led back to the first floor,[14] but there is no way of knowing whether this staircase, which must have been similar to the 'imperial staircase at John Carr's Lytham Hall, was original.

CHAPTER FIVE

Work at Lancaster and Chester Castles, 1784–1815

A. General Introduction – Georgian prisons

Harrison's clock tower at the City Museum and his spire at St John's Church are passed by thousands every day, but the most important of his works in Lancaster – the Gaol and Courts, which he designed for the County authorities in the Castle – are seen much less often. The same is true of Chester, where he was working at the same time.

Unless one studies Harrison's work at Chester and Lancaster together, it is easy to assume that his work at Lancaster preceded his work at Chester by a number of years, since almost all his buildings at Lancaster are earlier than almost any of his *surviving* buildings at Chester. However, Harrison produced his first designs for work at Chester *before* he began serious designing in Lancaster, and thereafter his works at Chester and Lancaster were exactly contemporary. This was to cause problems: considerable ones for him then, and lesser ones for us now, as we try to understand how the work on both sites was inter-related. This linking of the works was not a matter of chance: the magistrates in every County in the 1780s were thinking about the organisation of prisons, because life in Georgian gaols was generally somewhat disorganised.

The reasons for this lay not so much in the shortcomings of individuals, as in the way that the role of gaols had been expanded over the years, without much thought, in response to changing pressures. County gaols had originally been established in the Middle Ages to provide no more than short-term accommodation for only two groups of people – those awaiting trial at the twice-yearly Assizes, and convicted criminals who were waiting for their sentences to be carried out; this could be by hanging or, later, by transportation to an overseas colony. In the late-seventeenth century these people were joined by debtors – men and women with cash-flow problems, who could avoid formal bankruptcy by forfeiting their freedom until their finances improved. During the eighteenth century numbers were again increased by a third group – long-stay 'felons'. These were convicted criminals who had not been sentenced to death but could not, for various reasons, be transported or punished in a local house of correction (which corresponded roughly to a modern prison). Perhaps, though, the worst feature of Georgian county gaols – by our standards, but also, increasingly, by those of thinking people then – was that little attempt was made to segregate prisoners according to their category: debtors and people on remand awaiting trial were often mixed up with convicted criminals.

Responsibility (to the King) for the good order of a county gaol lay with the High Sheriff, but the County's JPs also had the right to inspect the premises. They were all, generally, humane men, but they had few ideas about what steps to take, and not enough time to study the problems and discuss solutions. Little progress was made until a remarkable man, John Howard – the 'patron saint' to this day of penal reform – had done just this. He was a Bedfordshire JP and was made High Sheriff in 1773. He persuaded Parliament to pass two Acts in 1774, which laid down that prisoners should be segregated according to their sex and category, that they should have communal day rooms but single cells for sleeping, and that sanitation and ventilation should be improved in the hope of reducing 'gaol fever'. (We now call it typhus and know that it is passed on by the bites of body lice, but it was then believed to be transmitted through damp, stale air.) In 1776 Howard published a book called *The State of Prisons*, and thereafter spent several months of each year, visiting and revisiting prisons in England and on the Continent, to encourage every authority to adopt the standards of the best. He visited Lancaster in 1776 and 1779 and was reasonably satisfied by what he saw. He went to Chester in 1784 and compared part of it to the Black Hole of Calcutta. He died in 1790, of gaol fever – in Russia.

As a result of Howard's campaigning, a competition was organised to obtain ideas for the design of a new building type, a long-stay prison called the National Penitentiary, in London. The competition was won in 1782 by the architect, William Blackburn, who was later to contribute ideas to the designs of the gaols in both Lancaster and Chester. In fact, little was done anywhere until after 1783, when a nation-wide outbreak of typhus killed some judges and JPs, and also the Keeper of Lancaster Gaol. This epidemic stimulated Parliament to pass a general Act in 1784, encouraging JPs to apply for private Acts, which would allow them to rebuild and enlarge county gaols.

B. Harrison's first involvement in Lancaster and Chester, 1784–86

The Lancashire JPs had already set up a Committee after the Summer Assizes in 1783 'for making and prosecuting the Improvements agreed upon and directed to be done at the Castle of Lancaster', but Harrison's name did not appear in its official records until 3 October 1786, when it was decided 'to procure plans, if necessary, from Mr Harrison'.[1] It is clear from diaries and letters, quoted by Ockrim,[2] that he had been involved in meetings in September 1784 and November 1785. However, it is difficult to avoid the conclusions that the Lancashire JPs were not really convinced of the need for action, and also that they had too many advisors – not merely William Blackburn, who was by then a friend of John Howard, but also two local JPs with an interest in prison design. These were Thomas Butterworth Bailey, who had been High Sheriff in 1768 and was the Chairman of the JPs in Quarter Sessions, and Roger Dewhurst, who made a study of Lancashire prisons in 1784. The JPs seem to have thought that they could design the gaol by themselves, since the phrase 'if necessary' in the minutes of 3 October 1786 comes after the approval of plans already provided by Dewhurst.

There was never an overall plan for the development of a new county gaol in Lancaster Castle. Harrison produced piecemeal plans, firstly under the inspection of Dewhurst in July 1787 (at an estimated cost of £3,626) and then amended plans (without any mention of Dewhurst and at an estimated cost of a further £5,117) in July 1788, after the Lancashire JPs had obtained their Act of Parliament. It had already been agreed in July 1787 that Harrison should supervise the work for a fee of £210 – later raised to £350 – and have until Michaelmas (September) 1790, or 1791, to complete the works. This contract for the initial works was later extended until 1792. Further schemes, and then delays in construction, led to further extensions until 1796 and then July 1798.

* * *

On the south side of the Mersey the Cheshire JPs had started a year later – it was only at the Midsummer Assizes in August 1784 that they had decided that the county gaol was 'insufficient, inconvenient and in want of repair'. However, after discussions in October 1784 with William Blackburn, who had not approved of plans submitted by the local architect, Joseph Turner, they organised a proper competition in April 1785 for a new gaol in Chester Castle. It was won, with a prize of 50 guineas, by Harrison in February 1786, that is, six months or so *before* he began serious work on designs for Lancaster.[*] Indeed, it seems likely that Harrison's success in Cheshire was an important factor in his nomination by the Lancashire JPs, since the record in October 1786 mentions 'the approbation he has met with at Chester and other places in furnishing the most approved plans of gaols and prisons and having due regard to Oeconomy'.

As at Lancaster, the Castle at Chester in the 1780s was used as the County Gaol, as well as accommodating civil and crown courts. It was also the home of a small garrison, which meant that the Army had to be consulted over

---

[*] The runners-up in the competition were William Cole, a builder in Chester, and Hiram Haycock, the architect son of a builder in Shrewsbury, who went on to win the competition for the Shropshire County Gaol in 1787.

[Figure 12]
Chester Castle,
*c.*1775 by Moses
Griffiths. The
Shire Hall on the
far left hides the
sloping site on
which Harrison's
County Gaol was
to be built. All
that now remains
of the medieval
castle in the
background is
Agricola's Tower
on the left.

work on parts of the site. A number of medieval buildings remained there.
[Figure 12] Most of them surrounded the moated inner bailey – an Anglo-
Saxon fort, strengthened by William the Conqueror – while some were
scattered around the outer bailey. This was somewhat smaller than the
present entrance courtyard and still contained the Elizabethan Shire Hall,
used for the Assizes. Harrison's new Gaol was to be built on a new site
behind the Shire Hall. All that now remains of these medieval buildings is
the so-called Agricola's Tower, which was built around 1200 as the
gatehouse between the outer and inner baileys.

Little now remains of the county gaol, designed by Harrison for the site
which slopes steeply down to the River Dee. Some of the buildings were
demolished in 1901–2, and most of the rest went to make way for the
County Hall, begun in 1939. No more than a few barrel-vaulted cells, used
for refractory felons, still exist below and to either side of what was the
Gaoler's House. Several plans and drawings of Harrison's façades remain,
however, because the County authorities insisted in 1801 that he deposit
them with the Clerk to the Justices. As at Lancaster, there are also the
Minutes of the Committee of JPs, set up in September 1786 to oversee the
work.[3]

Harrison had begun to develop his plans for the Cheshire Gaol soon after
winning the competition in February 1786, and they clearly reflected the
advice of William Blackburn, which was based on a recent prison in Ghent
in Flanders. Harrison also had a wooden model made [Figure 13] which is
now in the care of the Cheshire County Museum Service. It shows how,
within the perimeter walls of the semi-octagonal site there would be three
big wedge-shaped exercise courtyards for felons, spread out fanwise so that
they could be, literally, overlooked from the Gaoler's House behind the

[Figure 13] Harrison's model of Chester's County Gaol, c.1790, showing the semi-circular roof of the new Shire Hall, between the two courtyards for debtors, and the Gaoler's House from which the lower exercise yards and the sleeping-cell blocks could be overlooked. Reproduced by courtesy of Cheshire Museums Service.

Shire Hall. Along the outer wall of each courtyard would be two storeys of six sleeping cells, each measuring about nine feet by seven, and accessed from a gallery, built above an arcade – to give shelter within the courtyard, but also to make escape more difficult. A day room, about 12 feet square, was planned in each of the outer corners of each yard.

Harrison's Gaol was a new complex on a clear site, so all its buildings followed the contemporary conventions of Classical design. Every façade was heavily rusticated, as the side wings of the Shire Hall block still are. This was a motif copied from George Dance's recent Newgate Prison in London – both to stress the inferior status of the prisoners' quarters and to suggest that escape was impossible through the massive walls. Depending on one's status within it, the Chester building must have been an impressive, or an oppressive, symbol of the power of the law. It certainly oppressed an actor, S.W. Ryley, imprisoned for debt in 1812, who wrote in his *Memoirs* (1816) 'The stupendous walls – the massy doors – the grated windows – all, everything I look at, reminds me of a bastille; and almost makes me ask whether I am not a criminal, incarcerated for some capital offence'.[4] The male debtors' courtyard survives in part within the present Crown Courts complex, and when one looks at its rusticated walls, it is easy to sympathise with Ryley's view.

The site was staked out in November 1786 to show the JPs the extent of the new works, but nothing could be done until an Act of Parliament had given them the powers to demolish and rebuild what was the King's castle. Harrison must have been pleased, when the County authorities also decided to demolish the old Shire Hall, which did not sit neatly with his plan for the gaol, and to replace it by one designed by him; the demolition work was not, however, begun until after the Summer Assizes of 1792.

The Act was passed in July 1788, and work began on the gaol soon after, since it was an urgently needed building. Harrison declined to supervise the contract, because he had enough to do in Lancaster – at Skerton Bridge and in the Castle – and had recently supplied the plans for St Mary's Bridge in Derby. It was therefore decided to engage William Bell, an architect from Wrexham, at a salary of £200 per year. In November 1788 he and Harrison began to lay the foundations of the perimeter wall – a largely symbolic gesture, since the lime mortars, then used, set slowly and are damaged by frost, so that no building work could be done in the winter.

By then serious building work had begun in Lancaster, and it is appropriate to look at this first.

C. Early Works in Lancaster, 1788–96

Unfortunately, none of Harrison's plans for Lancashire's county gaol has survived, and the indications of the progress of the building work in the records are somewhat sparse. Harrison's planning was tightly constrained by the existence on a fairly small site of substantial remains of the walls and

[Figure 14]
Lancaster Castle, 1778, showing the gaps on either side of John of Gaunt's Gateway, which were to be filled by Harrison's first buildings.

South VIEW of Lancaster CASTLE.

towers of the medieval castle, between which he had to build. [Figure 14] The most visible remains now are the impressive John of Gaunt's Gatehouse and the Well Tower, which stands about 30 yards to its right. Behind them stands the great twelfth-century Keep, whose top storeys can be seen from the grounds of the Priory Church. Since all Harrison's new works were going to be placed *between* medieval buildings, he proposed to use what were then called 'Gothick' motifs, like battlements and pointed windows, at least in the main facades of his buildings. (There is a drawing for Chester Castle, which shows that he was toying with the same idea there, although nothing came of it.)

There was nothing strange about using such motifs. It was an approach adopted mainly out of courtesy towards work close at hand – as Henry Sephton's tower at St Mary's Church, finished in 1755, had been; there may also have been a wish to allude to the medieval origins of the English legal system. Harrison made no attempt, however, to replicate medieval work, let alone to produce something, which might be thought to be authentically medieval. Such an approach, epitomised in the work of Augustus Pugin, was rare before the late 1830s.

Work began in 1788, and the first building to be finished – in 1789 – was the **Keeper's House**, which stands just to the right of the Gatehouse. Its entrance was altered towards the end of the nineteenth century, but the original four-storey, tower-like central block can still be clearly seen, with its pointed windows. Its basic form – a tower with a flat face to the outside world and a semi-octagonal front to the courtyard, so that the Keeper could see at least something of life in the gaol – was the model for all the other prison buildings which Harrison was to design at Lancaster.

Although the Keeper's House has long been converted into offices for prison staff, its interior still retains a little of its original character as a sort of town house, with its reception rooms on the first floor to raise them above the prison courtyard. The major doorways and other openings have pointed heads, and the main rooms have good cornices and shutters to the windows.

After the completion of the Keeper's House the next significant work was the **Female Felons' Prison**, which was built in 1792 to comply with the law of 1774 and to segregate men and women prisoners. It stands immediately to the left of the Gatehouse, in a four-storey tower with square-headed windows, which can just be seen from outside above the wall. This tower also has a semi-octagonal front with Gothick windows to the courtyard, and so roughly matches the façade of the Keeper's House – making a symmetrical group centred on the Gatehouse.

At much the same time, to the south of the Keep, an attractive five-bay Gothick arcade – a plan probably derived from the felons' cells at Chester – was built to give some shelter for the debtors, who were to allowed to wander around the courtyard. Two storeys of further accommodation for

debtors were built above this arcade, probably in 1794, with domestic-looking, two-light windows. Needless to say, none of these buildings can be seen by the public, but most are visible in a drawing, made about 1824 by a debtor, James Weetman. [Figure 15]

When Harrison had reported on progress to the JPs in July 1792, his plans for a programme of major works were approved, and his contract was extended until July 1794. He was further allowed £650 – he never seems to have received an annual salary – 'as a satisfaction for the plans and models he has prepared and for the works he has already carried on and which is [*sic*] now expected to be executed'. These works included the **Male Felons' Prison**. However, work could not start until the medieval castle wall had been demolished and a more extensive area had been enclosed by a new high wall, built on land north of the Keep: one can see this on the plan of the Castle [Figure 16], published by Christopher Clark in 1807, in his *Account of Lancaster*.[5] This wall encloses a roughly semi-circular site, of much the same size as at Chester, but the arrangement is better: the site was divided fan-wise into four triangular courtyards, separated by walls, and radiating from a central point, where the two-storey turnkey's lodge stood; from here one warder could supervise the prisoners in all the yards.

Standing between each pair of courtyards two broad, battlemented, four-storey towers were built; they can be seen from outside, rising above the

[Figure 15]
Lancaster Castle: James Weetman's drawing of 1824, showing, to the left of the Keep, Harrison's debtors' wing and, to the right, the four-storey towers containing the male felons' sleeping cells, and the two-storey turnkey's lodge.

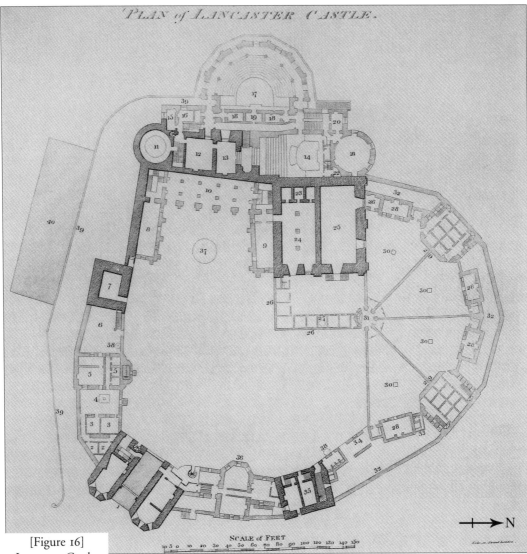

SCALE of FEET

[Figure 16]
Lancaster Castle:
Plan (1807) showing
Harrison's main
buildings – 36.
Keeper's House; 5.
Women's Prison
(and hospital); 10.
Debtor's Arcade and
accommodation; 31.
Turnkey's Lodge; 29.
Male Felons' Cells;
14. Crown Court;
and 17. Shire Hall.

walls. Inside the walls, they have broad semi-octagonal fronts to the courtyard. On each side they have barred Gothick windows – just visible to the outside world – but these light corridors, and not the cells themselves. These cells, which – as at Chester – measure about nine feet by seven feet and are eight feet high, were only used at night, when convicted prisoners slept alone. They are roofed with stone slabs and have iron doors to the corridors, which could be barred and locked, with a barred ventilation opening above them. [Figure 17] Such a plan and accommodation were typical of what was then regarded as the best current practice, advocated by Howard and Blackburn. Solitary confinement at night was not a dreamt-after privilege, but the normal practice – to encourage a convicted felon to examine his conscience in the hope that he would come to feel the need for repentance and reformation. Some of these cells still exist in the north-eastern tower, now used for prison storage. Visitors to the parts of the Castle, which are open to the public, can see a similar arrangement, during guided tours, in what are called the 'medieval dungeons' next to the lowest storey of Adrian's Tower.

The work of this second phase ran smoothly enough at the beginning. At the Quarter Sessions in January 1794 Harrison was ordered by the JPs to go to Gloucester to view the interior arrangements of William Blackburn's recently completed county gaol, which was widely regarded as a model. It was reported that the works at Lancaster had so far cost £10,853 – more than had been anticipated – and there were also complaints about delays. In April 1794 Harrison could not attend the Quarter Sessions. No explanation was given – it was in fact the only meeting he missed until 1797 – and his contract was extended until July 1796. There were, however, further complaints about delays in August 1794, and Harrison assured the JPs that the work would be finished by the Spring Assizes in 1796. He must have been able to keep to his undertaking, since the final bill for painting 64 iron doors – for 32 cells in each of the two towers – was paid in that year.

However, on 6 August 1795 the JPs learned with some consternation that Harrison had moved to Chester. Even in the terse language of the minutes – 'Information has been given that Mr Harrison … is removed to Chester and engaged in another employ and

[Figure 17]
Lancaster Castle: a Corridor in a Male Felons' Tower, with cells on the right, 2004.

therefore cannot give sufficient attendance at Lancaster' – it is clear that a bombshell had exploded. However, some of the JPs, on second thoughts, must have remembered that Harrison had won the Chester competition, and a number of Lancashire notables certainly knew that he was working in Chester. He was summoned to a meeting in October 1795, at which he undertook to complete the plans, which he had delivered, on or before 1 July 1797. These plans were for the Shire Hall and Crown Court – but before looking at them, it is appropriate to look again at what he had been doing in Chester.

D. Early Works at Chester, 1789–1802

Building work did not begin properly on the new Cheshire county gaol until the spring of 1789. By February 1790 Harrison was producing plans for buildings within the tall, semi-octagonal wall, which hid the gaol from the outside world. However, in August 1790 he had to be asked for detailed plans and sections of the felons' yards and the arcades, on which the rows of sleeping cells would be built. In 1791 he had also to be asked twice for plans for the Shire Hall and for the Gaoler's House, which projects behind it at the level of the present main courtyard, and for the two-storey Chapel below it. Work began on these in the spring of 1792, and by early 1794 the felons' prison was complete. Nothing significant of it now remains. Work on the debtors' accommodation at the upper level to the east and west of the Shire Hall had also been begun, but it was not completed until February 1801. Only the outer walls of these buildings now remain, but something of the gaol's original external appearance can be seen in an old print. [Figure 18]

At this time Harrison was still living in Lancaster, and his relationship

[Figure 18] Chester County Gaol, seen from across the River Dee, 1817.

with the Cheshire JPs 80 miles away – a long day's journey even in one direction – was not an easy one. They threatened him with dismissal in 1791 and 1792, if he did not send plans soon. There was, however, another side to the story: Harrison had been promised 50 guineas for his competition drawings in July 1786, but received nothing until July 1791, when he was also given £257 for his 'trouble and expenses to this time'. Furthermore, it was only in April 1792 that he was paid 30 guineas for the expenses of a journey to London in the summer of 1786. It is hardly surprising that, when he wrote to apologise to the JPs in April 1792, he added that he attributed his 'neglect of sending plans etc in some degree to a want of encouragement from the Commissioners or to an expectation that his services would not be properly compensated by them'. He clearly regarded himself as a professional man, entitled to reasonably prompt payment; they probably regarded him as a superior tradesman and were certainly displeased by his attitude, which lacked the proper respect owed to them as gentlemen.

1794 was a bad year for Harrison, since the way in which William Bell had run the job was being criticised. This was not Harrison's fault, of course, especially since in 1791 he had written two memoranda of advice on the use of stone in the new gaol. Nevertheless, he had to investigate the accusations, made against Bell – of wasting good Manley stone by using it for foundations, paying workmen more than agreed, destroying invoices, and leaving the Castle site unsupervised or under the care of an inexperienced nephew. He had to spend a full week in Chester at the end of April – which is why he missed the Quarter Sessions in Lancaster – and then he presented a report to the Cheshire JPs at the beginning of May. Not surprisingly, Bell was dismissed. Harrison was appointed as Surveyor of the works at the Castle on £400 per year – but only on the condition that he came to live in Chester and also employed a full-time foreman at his expense. He stalled as long as he could, but was eventually compelled, under pain of losing his job, to comply, although he did not move to Chester until the end of July 1795. These pressures may help to explain some of his actions in Lancaster.

Nevertheless, 1794 also saw him producing much of the detailed design work for the Shire Hall and ancillary accommodation for judges and juries and witnesses. Building work was, however, delayed by the need to remove and replace the foundations of the chapel, which had been laid by Bell but were inadequate. By August 1797, though, the outer walls of the Shire Hall were complete, but it was not until May 1798 that Harrison provided drawings for the ceiling. The building was roofed in 1799, but the interior work was not completely finished until 1802.

The **Shire Hall** is now the oldest building by Harrison in Chester Castle; however, since it is still used as a criminal court, it is seldom open to visitors. It is also one of the very earliest public buildings to use Greek motifs, and Giles Worsley calls it 'the first serious monument of the Greek Revival'.[6]

[Figure 19]
Chester: Interior of
the Shire Hall, as
originally used,
c.1835.

That term was not coined until 1842, and whatever it may have come to
mean subsequently, Harrison in his own mind was probably doing no more
than using some of the newly fashionable 'Grecian' motifs from the recently
extended 'antique manner' repertoire.

The Shire Hall has an impressive interior, but its acoustics have never
been satisfactory, and the original use of its space has been reversed and tall
screens have been placed between the columns. It is therefore difficult to
get a good feel of the courtroom, as designed. Fortunately, there is an old
print. [Figure 19] The room is in plan a semi-circle with a diameter of 80
feet. It was originally entered from the great courtyard through the portico,
and then to either side of the judges' bench, which stood on the straight
side, under a screen of two smooth-faced[*] Ionic columns – 22-foot
monoliths of Manley stone. In front of the curved wall stands a sweeping
range of ten similar columns, which separate the body of the court from
the outer circulation area and then carry an entablature from which the
ceiling rises to a height of 44 feet. This must be hung from the principal
roof trusses and has the form of a coffered semi-dome – a Roman, not a
Greek, motif – with a skylight at the top.

The main source of the design must have been the lecture theatre in
Jacques Gondoin's Ecole de chirurgie (now the Ecole de médecine) in Paris,
which created a sensation when it was completed in 1775 and which

[*] Columns in ancient Greece were nearly always fluted.

Harrison probably saw on his way home in 1776. Gondoin had clearly been inspired by the formula of Roman theatres, but had also closely copied details of another Classical work, the Pantheon in Rome, which, of course, Harrison knew well. In effect, he had created a sort of half-Pantheon – a quarter-sphere above a half-circle. Such a use of simple geometric shapes was very fashionable in France at the time, but Harrison did not copy Gondoin slavishly. Gondoin's theatre has a semi-circle of tiered seats rising to the outer wall, giving a clear view of the dissecting table on a low stage in the centre of the flat wall, and the dome rests on this outer wall. The Chester Shire Hall, however, has a semi-circle of columns *within* its outer wall, and they carry the dome and separate the actual courtroom from the surrounding public space.

Such copying of antique examples was fashionable from the 1770s – it was part of the attempt to find authoritative sources for contemporary design in the 'antique manner', mentioned earlier – but it sometimes created problems. In Italy the sun stands high in the sky and is often glaring – and even Paris in the north of France lies to the south of any part of England. A room, lit to an acceptable level in Rome, is consequently somewhat dark in Chester, even with a large window over the former judges' bench.

The **façade of the Shire Hall complex**, as seen from the entrance courtyard, is long and low – about 250 feet long but only 25 feet high, with nineteen bays and only two storeys. [Figure 20] The six-bay side wings, which originally served to screen the courtyards of the debtors' prison, are heavily rusticated – and even the lintels of the doors and windows are treated as flat arches, composed of five separate stones. In contrast, the strongly projecting seven-bay centre is built of ashlar, to emphasise the

[Figure 20]
Chester: Harrison's drawing of the proposed Shire Hall and its Portico (and the Armoury) *c.*1797. Reproduced by courtesy of Cheshire Museums Service.

dignified status of the Shire Hall. The centre has a high attic, but its main feature is the monumental, pedimented portico. This is designed in a simplified Greek Doric order, without the triglyph frieze, although the interior of the Shire Hall is in the Ionic order.

This portico was originally planned as a recessed portico – that is, with six monolithic columns in the line of the front wall – but by the time the first stone was laid in October 1797, it had been changed to have 12 columns and to project about ten feet in front of the rest of the building. These unfluted Doric columns are as high as the Ionic ones in the Shire Hall, but had, according to Classical conventions, to be significantly thicker. They rise straight from the pavement without bases. In contrast to the expressive rustication of the wings, this portico is a very austere work and is a fine example of the 'noble simplicity and quiet grandeur'[*] which were then regarded as the essential qualities of Greek art.

It is, moreover, probably the first façade of a public building in England – as distinct from a 'folly' in a gentleman's park, like Stuart's famous temple of 1758 at Hagley – to have a free-standing Greek Doric portico.[†] This very early use of Greek motifs in the Greek manner – somewhat unusual, though, since Greek Doric columns were normally fluted – is another measure of Harrison's importance in the history of English architecture. (Since he always used Greek Doric columns after this, the word 'Doric' will henceforth mean 'Greek Doric'.) The sheer scale of the portico, even today, evokes surprise at first sight and then admiration – and even awed appreciation among those of us who are associated with the building trades, since we can calculate that the columns must weigh well over ten tons. Harrison doubtless used their massive and sober forms to suggest the solemnity of the processes of the criminal law. His example was followed before long over the whole country – in town halls and hospitals too.

To all intents and purposes, the Shire Hall and County Gaol were complete by 1802, but by then the JPs were thinking of enlarging the outer courtyard of the Castle. However, before looking at this scheme, it is appropriate to return to Lancaster for the last time.

E. Last works at Lancaster, 1796–98

As work progressed on Lancashire's County Gaol in the early 1790s, it began to seem fitting to the authorities to do more – to rebuild the Crown Court

---

[*] The phrase was coined in 1764 by the German archaeologist, Johann Winckelmann, who had championed the Greeks against Piranesi.

[†] Free-standing Roman Doric porticos were not rare – Lancaster's Old Town Hall has one. There is a free-standing Greek Ionic portico, dating from 1771 at West Wycombe Park. There is a Greek Doric portico at the former County Gaol at Warwick, dating from 1779, but its columns are engaged, that is, part of the wall – as the Romans used them, but not the Greeks.

[Figure 21]
Lancaster: Shire
Hall from the
Castle Terrace,
1833.

and the Shire Hall, to make them worthy of the County Palatine of
Lancaster, whose Duke was the King himself. The Crown Court at
Lancaster was still held in the Castle's medieval Hall, while the Shire Hall,
used for civil cases, was in the Keep. Before new court buildings could be
erected, however, land had to be bought beyond the castle ditch to the west
and then surrounded by a high retaining wall to form a terrace. It was not
therefore until 1796 that the Hall, which stood to the south-west of the
Keep, was gutted. The walls of its basement still survive, and some can be
seen during guided tours of the Castle. Thereafter a new Crown Court and
Shire Hall were begun to Harrison's Gothick designs.

These form an impressive symmetrical group of buildings to the west of
the Keep, and were designed to be seen from the wide terrace, where they
compose well with the Keep or with the tower of the Priory Church. [Figure
21] Their layout can be seen at the top of Clark's plan [Figure 16] and their
interiors can also be visited as part of the public tour of the Castle. The
roughly semi-circular Shire Hall, with its tall traceried windows, projects
stongly between a refaced medieval round tower on the south (known now
as Adrian's Tower) and a new round tower on the north. This tower has
no name, but accommodates on the lower floor the so-called Drop Room,
from which, until 1865, felons were led through a sort of French window
to a scaffold outside, where they were hanged in public. Above the Drop
Room and lit by traceried windows, like those in the Shire Hall, is the

Grand Jury Room. This attractive circular room, which has a plaster vault springing from six corbels (and much of its original furniture, bought by the County authorities from Gillow's) is where – until the system was abolished in 1933 – the JPs met to decide whether the case against a prisoner was sufficiently strong for him or her to have to stand trial at the Assizes.

Work on the courts progressed slowly, partly because money was not readily available for major projects after the outbreak of war with the new French Republic, but in part because Harrison had moved to Chester and was trying to run the Lancaster scheme from there. (He was also working on a couple of country houses in Scotland – see Chapter 7.) The JPs were very angry, but they wanted the work to be finished and needed Harrison as much as he needed them. He had to admit in July 1797 that the Courts were not finished, and asked for another year. The duty of carrying out monthly inspections of the building work was then entrusted to Richard Threlfall, who had supervised the building of Skerton Bridge.

[Figure 22] Lancaster: Interior of the Shire Hall, c.2000. Reproduced by permission of Lancashire County Council.

The shell of the Crown Court was finished first, because it is a simpler building, constructed largely against the wall of the Keep, but the structure of the bigger, more complicated Shire Hall was not completed until July 1798. Both Courtrooms stand on the first floor, the normal arrangement for the main rooms of Georgian public buildings. The **Crown Court** – which is often used for criminal trials, but can be seen at other times – is a simple rectangular room about 50 feet long by 30 feet wide and high. It is lit from large windows in the upper part of the west wall and from an octagonal timber lantern with Gothick details in the flat ceiling.

The **Shire Hall** was designed a few years after the one at Chester and is clearly derived from it. [Figure 22] It is a splendid room – in plan half a polygon, about

80 feet in diameter – arresting at first sight and giving much to appreciate thereafter. Six slender free-standing Gothic piers in an approximate semicircle carry not merely most of the weight of the timber half-arches, which support the panelled 'vault' over the main part of the courtroom, but also the arches which separate the court from the surrounding aisle under its plaster vault. As originally in Chester, this is an attractive and ingenious solution, allowing the public to stand behind the arcade to watch the business of the court proceed in dignified surroundings.[*] Visitors still approach the Shire Hall from one side and then move through a curved space, looking slightly down on the court furnishings. The judges' bench with its elaborate Coade-stone canopies[7] is placed across the diameter of the room, under a great four-centred arch, panelled with tracery. It is without doubt a reworking in Gothick dress of the Shire Hall at Chester but is, in my view, finer. The vault arches rise directly from the piers, and the room is better lit by windows on the circumference, which catch the afternoon sun and allow the light to play on the forms of the piers and vaulting ribs. Furthermore, these windows are behind the public in the court – which makes the legal process more visible.

The structural shell of the Shire Hall was finished and roofed in July 1798, but this delay had been too great for the patience of the JPs. They thought that Harrison had not given adequate attention to their project: Threlfall had, for example, reported in January 1798 that neither Harrison nor his nephew – this is the first mention of John Harrison – had attended the works at Lancaster since August 1797. On 31 July 1798, therefore, with the bulk of the work complete, the members of the Lancaster Castle Committee 'resolved unanimously that Mr Harrison's Engagement with the County of Lancaster according to an Appointment made by himself expire this day'. Harrison was angry not to have his contract extended. At a meeting in August, although some of his drawings for windows in the Courts and Grand Jury Room were approved, he refused – even against a 'reasonable compensation' – to hand over the necessary working drawings 'to enable the Committee…to complete the work to Mr Harrison's design'.

In their turn the members of the Committee were angry; they thought that Harrison had too often re-worked the details of a design while it was being built. It is not difficult to see their point, for he was a perfectionist. He designed every element of the prisons, and most of those in the courts, in either stone or wrought or cast iron to minimise the risk of fire damage, and he specified large stones – normally 12 inches deep – laid with a minimum of mortar, to increase security. A typical staircase in the gaol, for example, is made of stone, with an iron handrail, and the stairhall is roofed

---

[*] In 1990, in a storeroom in the Castle, I found the wooden model of the Shire Hall, made for Harrison, so that he could take the roof off and explain to the JPs how his design would work. It has now been restored and will some day be put on public display.

[Figure 23]
Lancaster Castle: A Stairway in the Male Felons' Prison,
c.1990.

with a stone barrel vault and top-lit by a cast-iron lantern, carried on four layers of stone slabs, set across the corners. [Figure 23]

The JPs also thought that Harrison had delayed the production of working drawings unnecessarily. According to Threlfall, the details of the vaulted ceiling of the Shire Hall had not been ready in November 1797; as we have seen, things were as bad in Chester, and so the JPs were probably right. But, on the other hand, the Committee's records also suggest – unconsciously – that the authorities had allowed the project to grow without much thought for the cost; they also show that, since the County Treasurer did not make regular payments to Harrison, the latter had had in 1793 to spend his own money to get work done at all.[8] It is not surprising that relations were strained, and matters were not settled until August 1804. Harrison seems to have received about £1,500 for his work at the Castle, but it is not clear from the records how much the buildings cost, though Clark in 1807 gave an estimate of 'upwards of £40,000'.[9]

Despite their difficulties the JPs were well pleased with their new Castle and, after the Assizes in August 1799, commissioned a fashionable London artist, Robert Freebairn, to paint a dozen watercolours of the project, for presentation to George III. The external views suggest that the work was complete, but the interiors of the Crown Court and Shire Hall show – with surprising honesty – little more than the structural shells with a few fittings.[10]

When the Treaty of Amiens in 1802 brought a lull in the war with

Napoleon's France, more money became available, and so a young architect called Joseph Gandy, who had been trained by James Wyatt and had studied in Rome at the Academy of St Luke, was called in to complete the furnishings and interior decorations of the Crown Court and Shire Hall. Approval was given to his designs in March and August 1804, and so it is to Gandy that we owe the pretty decorative screens behind the judges' benches in the Shire Hall and Crown Court, and the panelled tracery of the windows there and in Adrian's Tower and the Grand Jury Room. (In 1816 a correspondent of *The Times* called the Shire Hall 'one of the most elegant and spacious halls of justice in Great Britain' and praised the way in which the courts 'harmonize beautifully with the style of the ancient structure which they complete and adorn.')[11]

F. Last works at Chester, 1802–1815

Since my aim is to write a largely chronological story, it might have been appropriate to stop this chapter on Harrison's work at the two Castles at the end of the last section and then go on to look at other buildings elsewhere. By 1802 he had already designed all his country houses and his two surviving secular buildings in Liverpool and Manchester (see Chapters 7 and 8). Nevertheless, his work at the Castles is such an important part of his *oeuvre,* and the designs of the buildings around the Courtyard at Chester are so closely linked to the Shire Hall that the Chester narrative will continue here. Readers should, however, bear in mind that the buildings, described in Chapters 9 and 10, were also being designed at the same time as those in this section. (They may also find it helpful to refer to the chronological list in Appendix A.)

The interior decoration of the Chester Shire Hall was finished in 1802, but completion of the Grand Jury Room and others in the wing to the west was delayed unavoidably. In consequence, Harrison's salary as Surveyor was stopped in September 1803, but fortunately for him, he had other schemes in progress elsewhere. Thought had already been given to the creation of a parade ground for the Castle's garrison, surrounded by imposing buildings, and so he continued to produce drawings. He was re-instated in August 1807, with a back-payment of £400 and £75 for travelling expenses, plus the promise of £400 per year – which was honoured – until the scheme was completed in 1815.

The first building for the parade ground, which he designed in 1804, was a new **Armoury** on the west side. He then designed a matching block for the other side of the courtyard, to serve as the front for a much larger complex of utilitarian buildings, first used as a **Barracks** (and now as a regimental museum). [Figure 24] Before work could start, an agreement about costs had to be reached with the government's Board of Ordnance: the County paid for the front and end walls (which are visible) and the

[Figure 24]
Chester: The
Barracks at the
Castle, 2004.

government paid for the rest. Work on these buildings was delayed for a couple of years, as the County was short of money, but was probably finished in 1810, which is the date on a rainwater hopper.

Each of these two buildings is a two-storey wing of nine bays, decorated by giant Ionic half-columns, unfluted monoliths some 23 feet high. Harrison intended to design these wings 'uniformly with the gaol of the Castle'[12] and originally gave them each a four-column portico around the central doorway. In the final design, however, the strong vertical emphasis of the half-columns is countered by the band between the storeys, the cornices of the lower windows and the frieze, which together draw one's eyes towards the Shire Hall. These columns have the Ionic order of the interior of the Shire Hall, rather than the Doric of its very visible portico. I can only explain this inconsistency by assuming that Harrison wished these buildings to be subservient to the main axis of the courtyard, which runs between the austere Doric portico of the Shire Hall and the imposing Doric entrance gateway.

The rest of the courtyard is surrounded by curved walls, topped with the original geometric railings. Joseph Farington visited Chester on 20 September 1808 and found the courtyard 'very spacious and of good form', but many people feel that the sense of enclosure is somewhat slight, and that the courtyard is too extensive for the height of the buildings around it. However that may be – and the dimensions were more or less imposed on Harrison – there can be no doubts about the magnificent **Propylaea Gateway**. The first stone was laid in June 1811, the first fluted Doric columns – a form which Harrison had already used in the Manchester Exchange in 1806 (see page 84) – were raised in August 1813, and work was finished in 1815.

Harrison had been producing designs for this gateway since at least 1808.

[Figure 25]
Chester: Harrison's
first design for the
Castle Gateway,
c.1808. Reproduced
by courtesy of
Cheshire Museums
Service.

One of his earlier drawings [Figure 25] shows a sort of triumphal arch, with paired Doric columns and full entablature extending to form a screen on either side, and terminating in a block, crowned with a shallow dome.[13] This drawing must have been seen by Farington, since he included a hint of it in a rough sketch of the courtyard in his diary. Harrison's final design was, however, based on the Propylaea on the Acropolis in Athens, which had been illustrated in Stuart and Revett's *Antiquities*. It has been suggested that the idea may have come from the Brandenburg Gate in Berlin, which the Earl of Elgin, Harrison's client at Broomhall (see page 71) had seen while he was ambassador to the Prussian court; or it may have been inspired by the (never built) Doric gateway, which William Wilkins designed in 1806 for Downing College in Cambridge. Both models are, in my view, unlikely. The Propylaea Gateway is not just one of the numerous Doric porticos, applied to country houses and public buildings on the model of the Chester Shire Hall; it was a sort of triumphal arch, raised after Napoleon's defeats in Russia and Spain; moreover, Harrison also put his own – almost a Palladian – stamp on the design, with its centre and pavilions. [Figure 26]

The central entrance block has on its outer side a double colonnade of four monolithic Doric columns, 18 feet high. They carry a triglyph frieze, topped with a low attic, with a taller central panel which was intended to carry an inscription commemorating British victories. The fluting of the columns is stopped in the bottom five or six feet.[*] The central block with

(*) This sensible detail was adopted in the light of the discussions in 1808 about the Northgate at Chester – see page 94.

[Figure 26]
Chester: Harrison's
final design for the
outer face of the
Castle Gateway,
*c.*1810. Reproduced
by courtesy of
Cheshire Museums
Service.

[Figure 27]
Chester: George
Cuitt's etching of
the inner face of
the Castle Gateway,
1815.

its double portico projects some ten feet in front of the two side pavilions, which served originally as guardhouses. These are lower and flat-fronted and have simple pediments, carried on two fluted Doric half-columns between pilasters. Towards the courtyard [Figure 27] the treatment is, however, reversed and the effect heightened, in that the pavilions now each have four fluted Doric columns and project ten feet further into the courtyard than does the central block, which has only two columns between pilasters.

Though the Propylaea is less tall and thus less immediately impressive than the Brandenburg Gate – which was, after all, a gate in the Prussian capital, not in a smallish county town – it is much more three-dimensionally dramatic. With its 22 monolithic columns, its massive beams supporting deeply coffered 'ceilings', its concentrated play of projection and recession, light and shadow, and its differing treatment above the entablatures, it is a gigantic piece of sculpture, through which one can walk and appreciate its structure. It is a work of national, and probably international, significance, and Piranesi would doubtless have been proud to have designed it.

These buildings, which Harrison designed around the courtyard of Chester Castle, are by common consent 'one of the most powerful monuments of the Greek Revival in the whole of England'. [Figure 28] The words are Pevsner's,[14] but their spirit is echoed in comments by other specialists in eighteenth-century architecture. Colvin goes furthest in his praise and says: ' [the] Chester Castle complex of buildings forms the finest group of Greek Revival buildings in Britain – the neo-classical counterpart to Greenwich Hospital'.[15]

The Castle was described in glowing terms in 1831 in the *History of the City of Chester*, written by Harrison's friend, Joseph Hemingway, but very few contemporary responses by *architects* to Harrison's work survive. The famous John Soane (who did not know Harrison then) saw the Shire Hall in 1810 and thought that it did its architect 'great credit'.[16] In November 1823 the young, and soon to be famous, architect, Charles Cockerell, who had long admired Harrison's work, visited Chester and met Harrison. In his diary he criticised Harrison's use of different orders – Doric, Ionic and

[Figure 28] Chester Castle Courtyard, *c.*1860. Reproduced by permission of the Grosvenor Museum, Chester City Council.

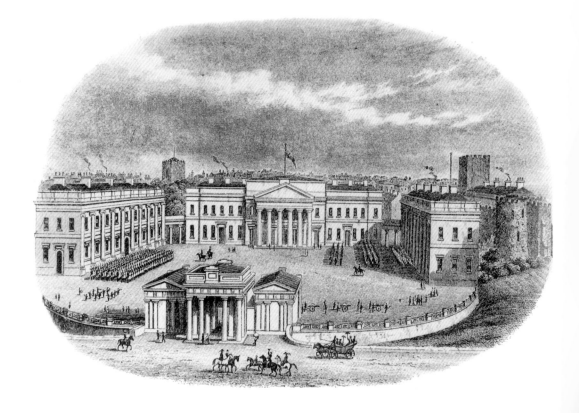

then a richer Doric – in what is, essentially, one scheme. Nevertheless, despite these reservations – which may seem to us pedantic, but are certainly justified by the conventions of his time – Cockerell's attitude was one of almost unstinted praise: 'Here a great hand is visible...It is in the great intelligence of the masonry that Harrison's merit lies'. Five years later he wrote: 'Harrison is undoubtedly the noblest genius in architecture we have had – in external architecture chiefly'.[17]

G. Harrison's Work at the two Castles – a Comparison

Harrison had to leave his work at Lancaster to be completed by other hands, but he lived long enough to finish his scheme at Chester Castle – although it is now incomplete. How do the two ensembles compare? But how does one compare chalk and cheese? Harrison chose to design in the Gothick manner at Lancaster, but used the conventional Classical design principles at Chester. As a competent architect of his day, he was at home in either style; there was no ideological 'battle of the styles' until Pugin's religious mania made architecture a matter of morals rather than of aesthetics.

Lancaster has, in my view, the more beautiful of the two Shire Halls, but the Propylaea at Chester is superb, and the ensemble of gateway, courtyard and Shire Hall portico is more magnificently dramatic than anything Harrison designed in Lancaster – even the view of the Shire Hall from the terrace. If, however, the Lancaster courtyard were ever cleared of its prison-derived clutter, most of us would probably find the walk through John of Gaunt's Gatehouse into the irregularly shaped and slightly rising courtyard, surrounded by the succession of Harrison's (and Gandy's) buildings, culminating in the medieval Keep, more impressive and more dramatic, but in a different – more informal, more picturesque – way. Harrison's work at Chester is like a grand piano sonata, but at Lancaster it is the solo part in a splendid concerto.

I doubt, however, that Harrison would have shared this view. He was a man of the mid-eighteenth century, trained in Rome and prepared to accept the straitjacket of symmetry. Our perceptions, on the other hand, are largely shaped – still – by the late-eighteenth-century reaction against formal Classical design and by the consequent preference for 'Picturesque' irregularity. Harrison himself was, to some extent, affected by this change in taste, as it occurred. We shall see this in the designs of some of his buildings, which have two different but adjacent façades, meant to be seen in one view; and also in most of his presentation drawings, which show buildings in a diagonal perspective – the normal way after about 1780. Nevertheless, however they are presented, each of these individual façades is strictly symmetrical in its design. Harrison must have been prouder of his work at Chester than of what he had designed at Lancaster, since he was content that the Propylaea Gateway should appear in the background of most portraits of him. [Frontispiece]

CHAPTER SIX

Thomas Harrison 'of Chester'

When Thomas Harrison, under pressure from the Cheshire JPs, left Lancaster in 1795, he was a man who had just turned 50 with a wife and three children. He must have left with some trepidation, but Chester had much to offer as a base for an architect with several major projects to his credit. It was a bigger and more important town than Lancaster, with a population of 15,000, compared with Lancaster's 9000, and a wealthier hinterland. It was also a cathedral city – Lancaster was in its diocese – as well as a county town, and had therefore more lawyers, clergy and professional men. Lancaster had recently been hit by unlucky losses of merchant ships in the wars with France, and there were signs that earlier hopes of significant development would not be realised. There even was talk of making Preston the seat of the County authorities, and this happened in fact in 1798. On the other hand, Chester was already the 'capital' of North Wales and was close to the growing towns of Liverpool and Manchester. A man with a practice there might also gain access to the West Midlands and thence, perhaps, to the Home Counties and London.

As Lancaster had been in the early 1780s, so Chester was in the mid-90s – a town without a significant practising architect. There was, to be sure, William Cole, the runner-up to Harrison in the competition for the county gaol, but he was primarily a builder. There was also Joseph Turner, but, fortunately for Harrison, he had stopped designing by 1795. If he had continued to practise, he would have provided Harrison with some stiff competition, for in Chester alone he had designed the long terrace on the west side of Nicholas Street in 1781 – described then as 'handsome brick buildings in the London style' – and both the Watergate and the Bridgegate in 1778 and 1792 respectively. He had also made designs for several buildings, both private and public, in North Wales.[1]

We know little of Harrison's 30 years of professional life in Chester. He worked at first from home, but had an office in the Shire Hall from 1805 until 1815, when his work there stopped. He presumably owned all the standard works on architectural practice – the more scholarly books by Gibbs and Ware, and also Peter Nicholson's *Student's Instructor* and the several books by Batty Langley, which were intended for craftsmen. It is known that he attended the sale of Sir William Chambers' library in 1796 and that he bought there a French edition of Vitruvius, and works on architecture by Palladio and the French architect, Jacques Blondel. His practice was never large, and he did not build his own house until the end of his life.

It is difficult in an age where faxes, e-mails, mobile phones and computer-aided design are commonplace to think ourselves back to a time when it was impossible to travel at more than an average speed of ten miles an hour, when drawings had to made with a pen, using ink from an inkwell, and when copies could only be made by pricking the main outlines of an original drawing through to a sheet of paper underneath it and then joining up the holes on the lower sheet. An architect with no more than one assistant or senior pupil could easily take on more work than he could cope with, but self-employed people fear famines more than feasts.

Harrison had been born in 1744, but in his approach to professional practice he was a man of the nineteenth century, refusing financial involvement with the contractors for the buildings which he had designed; this had been common practice in much of the eighteenth century. He sought, as Colvin put it, the 'social status and respectability … of a gentleman, a scholar and an artist',[2] a man to whom his employer could entrust his affairs with the same confidence as to his solicitor. He would no doubt have accepted the opinion of John Soane, who had written in 1788: 'The business of the architect is to make the designs and estimates, to direct the works, and to measure or value the different parts; he is the intermediate agent between the employer, whose honour and interest he is to study, and the mechanic [= craftsman], whose rights he is to defend. His position implies great trust: he is responsible for the mistakes, negligences, and ignorance of those he employs; and above all he is to take care that the workmen's bills do not exceed his own estimates.'[3]

It is easy to state one's position; it is more difficult to persuade others to accept it. For most of Harrison's lifetime, most of an architect's clients were land-owning gentlemen, who for the most part believed that architects, because of their obvious links with the building trades, were little better than tradesmen. Some of them, who knew a particular architect well and regarded his work highly, might have been prepared – but in that case only – to consider him a sort of gentlemanly tradesman, like a doctor. But such gentlemen were rare.

The delays in paying Harrison for work done at Kendal and at the Castles in Chester and Lancaster have already been mentioned, but they were not the only cases. Clergymen do not appear in any better light than laymen in this regard. After the building work at Whittington church was complete in 1804 (see page 87), Harrison sent in a bill for £40 for his design work and journeys to supervise the work; this was cheap for a building which had cost £1,500. In February 1811 he reduced this bill to £30 at the request of Rev. W.W. Davies, who had been the rector and was also a friend, but he was still not paid until June 1812. A more egregious instance concerns the design work, which he did for Chester Cathedral in 1819 (see page 88). His fee of £25 for his surveys and drawings was not paid until after his death ten years later, and then only when his executors requested it.

* * *

In 1795 there was no architectural profession in the provinces, in the sense of older men who trained younger men in the art and science of architecture. By the time of Harrison's death in 1829 that was, however, changing. In the late 1790s and early 1800s he employed his nephew, John Harrison, who acted as the clerk of works at Broomhall (see page 71) and also designed some ceilings for Gosford House at the same time.[4] Colvin attributes to John Harrison the designs of Sherdley Hall, near St Helens, in 1806 and the Synagogue in Seel Street, Liverpool in 1807. He calls them both 'competently designed classical buildings',[5] but both have been demolished. John Harrison drops out of the records soon after, but no-one knows why.

Harrison's principal pupils, according to Colvin, were John Hargrave, of Cork, Thomas Penson and then William Cole. None was a greater architect than he. Hargrave was the son of Abram Hargrave, who had worked on Skerton Bridge and whom Harrison had recommended to the Bishop of Derry. According to the *Dictionary* of the Architectural Publishing Society, he designed churches, country houses and gaols in most parts of Ireland. Thomas Penson was the son of an architect and building contractor in Wrexham. He was a pupil of Harrison's from about 1805 and then established his practice in Oswestry, as both an architect and civil engineer. He had a son, Thomas Mainwaring Penson, who became an architect and began the revival of timber framing in Victorian Chester.

William Cole was closer to Harrison than was Penson, and stayed on longer in Chester. He was the third man of that name to play a part in Harrison's life. He was the grandson of the builder whom Harrison had beaten in the Castle competition in 1786, and the son of the man who built several of Harrison's designs. He became Harrison's pupil in 1814 and succeeded him as County Surveyor in 1829. Like Harrison and most architects of his time, he could design, as required, in the Classical or the Gothick idiom: in 1829 he designed the attractive Bolesworth Castle, which is reminiscent of Harrison's Citadel at Hawkstone (see page 118), but in 1834 he drew the plans for the Methodist New Connexion Chapel in Pepper Street, Chester, with its sumptuous Corinthian portico.[6]

Ockrim states that around 1810 Harrison had another pupil, Thomas Jones, whose first commission – Talacre Hall, Flintshire – is somewhat similar in style to Hardwick Grange (see page 115). He went on to practise chiefly in North Wales. Documents relating to Harrison's work at Magdalen College, Oxford, and at the Grosvenor Bridge in Chester suggest that after about 1820 he also had an assistant called George Latham, who later set up practice as an architect in Nantwich.

In a minor way Harrison was also able to exercise patronage, as Sir Lawrence Dundas had done for him 35 years before. In 1804 he encouraged George Cuitt, the son of the friend, with whom he had travelled to Rome, to apply for a job as a drawing master in Chester. Cuitt got the job and lived in Chester until his father died in 1818. He is now known for his striking etchings, full of Piranesian light and shadow, including the attractive illustrations of Chester Castle Gateway and of St Nicholas' church in Liverpool, reproduced in this book.

CHAPTER SEVEN

Country Houses, 1793–1802

Harrison's minor works in Lancaster, and his major projects in the Castle there and in Chester kept him occupied until well beyond 1800. It is sometimes difficult for us to keep track of his work. It must have been worse for him, since in the crucial years 1793–98, when he was under pressure from the JPs in both counties, he was not only supervising work on Stramongate Bridge at Kendal, but was also producing designs for three country houses in the area around Edinburgh – Broomhall, Gosford, and Kennet House – as well as, almost certainly, for Quernmore Park Hall, near Lancaster. Another house – Colinton House, on the outskirts of Edinburgh – was to follow in 1801.

The ambition of every up-and-coming Georgian architect was to design a 'seat' for a wealthy and well-connected gentleman. This was not merely such a man's home and the administrative centre of his estate and the focus of his power within the locality, but also an expression of his status, whether aspired-to or acknowledged, and a symbol of his taste and authority. A couple of local successes in this field might lead an architect to more lucrative commissions from patrons of greater – even national – importance.

However, most of Harrison's early country house commissions were not local. The job at Quernmore is easy to understand – it stands three miles from Lancaster and its owner was a Lancashire gentleman – but how can one explain Harrison's works in Scotland? How did he get to know his clients, or – rather – how did they come to hear of him?

I used to think that the probable answer involved Sir Thomas Dundas, the son of his first patron, who had been unable to help him after his return from Italy. As his father had done, Dundas lived part of the year in Edinburgh, where he knew everyone who mattered. However, it now seems more likely that Harrison's first commission in Scotland came in 1793 from Francis Charteris, the seventh Earl of Wemyss, who lived at **Gosford,** on the south coast of the Firth of Forth a dozen miles east of Edinburgh. Charteris had links with the Lancaster area. Before inheriting his title and estates in 1787, he had owned the Hornby Castle estate, which he had inherited through his mother, Janet Charteris.[1] He seldom visited Hornby, but his brother, James Wemyss, acted as his agent there.

Harrison was first mentioned in the seventh Earl's cash books on 16 September 1793, when Joseph Bower, the clerk of Robert Adam (who had

[Figure 29]
Gosford: Harrison's
drawing for the
proposed
Mausoleum, *c.*1793.
Reproduced by
courtesy of
Cheshire Museums
Service.

designed Gosford in 1791 but had died in 1792), was paid five guineas 'for copying some of Mr Harrison's plans and drawing some working plans for the house at Gosford'. Harrison was mentioned again on 18 November 1794, when he was paid £31.10.0 'in full of all demands for the plan he made for the Alteration of Mr Adam's plan for Gosford House.'[2] His alteration cannot have been very significant, since his fee would have equated to no more than £700 of building work. Probably nothing now remains of Harrison's work at Gosford, since the house was substantially remodelled in the nineteenth century and badly damaged by fire in 1940. Gosford is still the home of the present Earl and is not open to the public.

Harrison clearly produced two sets of drawings – one for the alteration to Adam's plan in 1794, and one for something else in 1793. There is no way of knowing with certainty what this earlier scheme might have been, since there is no documentary proof. However, while looking through the Gosford drawings at the National Monuments Record of Scotland, I came across a photograph of a building, which reminded me of an attractive presentation drawing [Figure 29] in the collection of the Cheshire Museums Service at Northwich[3] – one of the drawings given by Anne Harrison to the Chester Archaeological Society in 1849 – and this suggests that Harrison's first job in Scotland was almost certainly the **mausoleum** in the private grounds of Gosford.

The mausoleum was designed to accommodate the body of the seventh Earl of Wemyss and was built between 1795 and 1798,[4] at a cost of about £1,100. [Figure 30] It is an austere square building of ashlar stonework, standing in the centre of large circular enclosure, planted with yew trees. It

[Figure 30]
Gosford: The
Mausoleum, 2005.

is about 30 feet each way and 15 feet high, and is capped by a pyramid, which rises to about 30 feet. On each side there is a portico of four Tuscan columns without bases, though only one contains an entrance. Its interior is octagonal and covered by the sloping sides of the pyramidal roof.[*] It is a good example of the fashion for pure geometry of that time. It bears no resemblance to two mausolea in Scotland, which Adam designed in 1790, but corresponds very closely to the drawing at Northwich.

An attribution to Harrison cannot be made with certainty, but this circumstantial and documentary evidence is, in my view, convincing beyond reasonable doubt. It seems probable that James Wemyss, while at Hornby, had seen and been impressed by Harrison's works at Lancaster and that, when his brother wanted an architect to design a mausoleum, put his name forward. It is furthermore likely that Harrison produced the

---

[*] Pyramids had long been regarded as one of the perfect geometric forms, and there is one in the park at Castle Howard, designed in 1729. Pyramidal tombs were just becoming fashionable in 1793. The Egyptians had, of course, used them, and some Romans had adopted the practice. Harrison must have seen the most famous example, the Pyramid of Gaius Cestius in Rome, which stood by the Protestant cemetery there. More recently, Joseph Bonomi had designed a simple pyramidal mausoleum at Blickling, which was built in 1792 for the Earl of Buckinghamshire. A very elaborate (and then well-known) mausoleum, designed by James Wyatt in 1783 for the Earl of Darnley, stands near Cobham Hall in Kent; it has a square base surrounded by Roman Doric columns and is capped by a pyramid. The seventh Earl of Wemyss was a freethinker and a prominent Freemason and wanted a tomb without Christian associations;[5] the mausoleum at Gosford is perhaps a very austere version of the one at Cobham.

[Figure 31]
Kennet House:
Entrance Façade,
1966. Crown
Copyright: Royal
Commission on the
Ancient and
Historical
Monuments of
Scotland.

presentation drawing, and maybe another which he took back to Chester, and also a sketch plan which was drawn up properly by Bower; and lastly that the Earl was satisfied enough with Harrison's ideas for a building in the garden to ask him to make the now lost alteration to the big house itself.

The Earl of Wemyss was a friend and neighbour of Sir Thomas Dundas in St Andrew's Square, Edinburgh, and it is a reasonable conjecture that, when Dundas' cousin, Alexander Bruce[*] needed an architect for his new house in 1793, Wemyss suggested Harrison. The house was **Kennet House** near Clackmannan. It was demolished in 1967, and this is probably the most significant loss from Harrison's *oeuvre*, since it was his first major house and contained many of the ideas, motifs and features, which were to appear in his later works. Fortunately, it was well recorded in 1966, with plans and many photographs, for the National Monuments Record of Scotland. Its quality was recognised immediately after its completion. Sir John Sinclair in his *Statistical Account of Scotland* (1795) stated that 'the only house in the parish of Clackmannan that deserves the name of elegant is just now finished by Mr. Bruce of Kennet, from a beautiful design of Mr. Harrison, of Lancaster.... It is also built in a style of superior elegance to most of the houses to be met with in Scotland'.

---

[*] Dundas' mother before her marriage had been Margaret Bruce of Kennet.

[Figure 32]
Kennet House:
Garden Façade,
1966. Crown
Copyright: Royal
Commission on the
Ancient and
Historical
Monuments of
Scotland.

The house stood on a low hill, with fine views northwards towards the Ochil Hills and southwards over the Firth of Forth. It was built across the contours of the site – like Carr's Harewood House – in such a way that the entrance façade of the house appeared to have a two-storey centre (above a half-hidden basement), while the south-facing garden-façade clearly had three storeys.

The general form of the house – spreading over the site – was typically Palladian and recalls the three houses at the end of Skerton Bridge. [Figure 31] The dimensions and details of the central block of the entrance façade, with its three wide bays, were similar to, and probably derived from, Springfield Hall at Lancaster. The door with its semi-circular porch, carried on four monolithic Tuscan columns, was flanked by tripartite windows – their mullions this time formed of Tuscan colonnettes – under a segmental relieving arch. The simple cornice of the porch's entablature continued across the windows and the whole of the façade – more neatly than at Springfield – to embrace the screen walls and pedimented pavilions. The horizontal lines of the façade were further emphasised by another simple cornice, which linked the sills of the upper windows. However, the windows on both floors were equally high – with 12-pane sashes, as at Springfield – and this redressed the balance.

The horizontal lines continued across the south-facing garden façade, but there were several elements, which gave a pleasingly strong vertical emphasis to the design. [Figure 32] The central block clearly had three storeys, and its central feature was a newly fashionable, full-height shallow bow; the main-floor windows had separate cornices, which made them appear slightly taller; and the side pavilions – here two-storeyed – had shallow, square bays with a simple tripartite window on each floor.

The plan of the main floor was typical of the period but, more specifically, was very close to Carr's plan for the long-demolished Wiganthorpe Hall, near York, which was built about 1778.[6] Towards the back of the entrance hall there was a three-bay screen of Tuscan columns, beyond which a central door led to the drawing room with its bowed end-wall. A door on the left led to the dining room, while the corresponding door on the right gave access to the stairhall and from there to the breakfast room, which was also linked to the drawing room. The staircase was built of stone and cantilevered around a wide open well; it had slender cast-iron balusters, and was lit from the side by a west-facing window.

All the rooms on all the floors were square or rectangular in plan, except for those in the bay. Although several rooms had fine fireplaces, decorative features were limited to good cornices, and plain architraves for six-panelled doors. Such austerity may have been requested by the client, but Harrison's later works suggest that it also corresponded to his taste.

Harrison's third country-house commission in Scotland, in 1795, must almost certainly have been due to the influence of Alexander Bruce of Kennet. It was to design major extensions at **Broomhall**, near Dunfermline, for his kinsman, Thomas Bruce, the seventh Earl of Elgin (who was also a friend of Dundas). The house is still the home of the present Earl and is not open to the public.

Harrison's commission was not an easy one. He was asked to extend and re-model an early-eighteenth-century house, in order to bring its appearance up to date. At that time it had slightly projecting ends, and a wing on both sides of the courtyard on the entrance front. He was also asked to keep the reception rooms on the first floor – which was no longer a fashionable arrangement. Harrison's plans arrived in March 1796, and the foundations of the new work on the south side were laid in April, but the design for the modernisation of the older part of the house was never finalised.

The story of the construction of the house provides an interesting case-study of the difficulties of building a major house, when the architect lives 250 miles from the site and the owner is in another country. Ockrim describes the process at length.[7] A major problem for Elgin was to find the money to match his aspirations to be a leader of architectural fashion. A major problem, as far as Harrison was concerned, was that Elgin was reluctant to make decisions about the several alternatives which he had been offered. (Among the many Harrison drawings at Broomhall are two variants for the north façade and no fewer than six for the south.) A further problem for Harrison was that Elgin also wanted changes, when work was in progress. For example, he did not want to install the large-paned French windows with bronze glazing bars which Harrison had suggested.[*] Nevertheless, the two men remained on good terms, and Elgin remembered Harrison in 1835 as 'the most classical and scientific architect of his day'.[8] This must be a tribute to Harrison's taste and technical skill.

Once the foundations of the southern extension had been laid, the main walls were built during the summer of 1796, but progress on the design of the rooms behind the façade was stalled, since Elgin had been sent to Berlin to serve as the Minister Plenipotentiary to Prussia in 1795. Little was done until he returned in 1798. Harrison's nephew, John, who had been the link between his uncle and Elgin's agent in Scotland, was appointed to be the site architect in November 1798. He left Broomhall in November 1799, when everything, which could be built to his uncle's approved plans, had been completed.[†] By this time Elgin had left again to be the Ambassador to the Court of the Ottoman Sultan in Constantinople (now Istanbul).

Elgin was the man to whom the British Museum owes the Elgin Marbles. Before he left for Constantinople, Harrison had expressed the hope that, while there, he would take the opportunity to collect Greek antiquities – since Greece was then part of the Ottoman Empire. Elgin went further than the making of drawings and plaster casts of sculptures and architectural ornaments, which Harrison must have meant. According to Canon Blomfield, he wrote to Harrison in November 1802, shortly before leaving Constantinople, saying: 'I feel a particular delight in acknowledging that I retain the greatest obligation to you, for having enabled me to do what has been done. For, I repeat it, it is you and you alone gave me the idea, and a notion of its importance'. Harrison's view of Elgin's *coup* is not on the record.

According to a pair of presentation drawings of about 1799 at Broomhall – which are unsigned but must be by Harrison and show the house from a diagonal viewpoint – his design was still traditionally Palladian with its two-and-a half storey central block, rusticated basement, and lower side wings. However, only the central block of the south front, facing the garden and a wide-ranging view over the Firth of Forth, was built as Harrison hoped.

---

[*] They were, however, introduced later and are there to this day with their original glass.
[†] Recent repair works showed how well built this part of the house was.[9] The ends of the tie-beams in the principal trusses in the roof were not built into the outer walls of the house, but rested on corbels, so that air could circulate around them. There were also no wooden lintels in the inner leaf of the walls above the windows; instead shallow stone rear-arches carried the weight of the wall above the openings. Such arches of stone or brick – a slightly more expensive but certainly stronger alternative to timber lintels – had long been traditional good practice in England and Scotland. Some can be seen in Harrison's Bridge Houses in Lancaster and at Grove House, Allerton, as well as in Adam's work at Gosford, so I surmise that the seventh Earl had the tie-beams in mind, when he called Harrison 'scientific'.

[Figure 33] It is an elegant design, built of the local sandstone. The central three bays and their roof swell out into a fashionable shallow domed bow with pairs of tall monolithic, Ionic half-columns on the main floor. These carry an entablature, whose cornice carries across the façade, but they also give a very necessary vertical emphasis in the rather wide front. The main-floor windows on the return walls are tripartite with Tuscan colonnettes, recessed under a segmental relieving arch.

[Figure 33] Broomhall: South Front, 2004.

Harrison's drawing of the south front shows – interestingly – two inaccuracies in the rendering of the perspective. [Figure 34] Firstly, the pavilion beyond the main block is clearly shown, although only part of it would have been visible from the point from which the rest of the drawing was made; that is probably no more than artistic licence. Secondly, however, the bowed front is inexpertly drawn, in such a way that its front edge appears to be higher than it is in reality.

The basement contained service rooms, and the reception rooms were kept on the raised main floor. This was the last time that Harrison designed a house in this old-fashioned way; henceforth his houses followed the contemporary pattern, with reception rooms on the ground floor. His designs put the dining room in the north-west corner, the drawing room in the south-west corner, and the library in the bow on the south. They form a fine suite of generously spacious rooms with tall windows, but the details of the interior décor were probably not designed by Harrison, since the house was not habitable until about 1810.[10] The top-lit main staircase is certainly by him, however; it rises to the right of the entrance hall and is cantilevered around a spacious open well.

[Figure 34]
Broomhall:
Harrison's drawing
for the South
Front, 1799.
Reproduced by
permission of the
owner.

Harrison's last commission in Scotland came in 1801. At the suggestion of James Bruce, Lord Elgin's brother, Sir William Forbes, a successful banker in Edinburgh, asked him (and four other architects) to produce designs for a large new villa, **Colinton House**, on an estate, which he had just bought south-west of Edinburgh. According to Colvin,[11] this procedure was still quite common in Scotland, though unusual in England. Colinton House is now in the suburbs of Edinburgh and has housed the science laboratories of Merchiston Castle School since 1931; it is not open to the public.

Forbes seems to have asked his agent, Richard Crichton,[12] to make an amalgam of what he thought were the best features of each design, though he later stated that most of them were Harrison's.[13] The main lines of the plan and elevations come from Harrison, though Crichton certainly made changes – there are a number of attractive features in the house, which appear here but not in Harrison's later works. Forbes managed the construction project through Crichton, with a separate contract with each of the major craftsmen. (This was no longer the normal practice in England.) The foundation stone was laid in April 1801 – before the design was finalised – and the work was completed in 1806. [Figure 35]

The house stands superbly on its site, on the top of a slope, which gives an extensive view northwestwards over the Firth of Forth, as far as Ben Lomond. The entrance front faces south; it has a pronounced cornice, five broad bays and two storeys above a half-hidden basement. It is rather like the centre of Kennet House without the tripartite windows – in my view an improvement – and is carried out with a refined elegance, which must be due more to Crichton than to Harrison. The porch, for example, is rectangular and carried on two pairs of Ionic columns, and the first-floor

[Figure 35]
Colinton House,
2004.

windows are tall enough to have 12-pane sashes. The centre of the rear façade is fashionably bowed and has a balcony on the main floor.

The interior of Colinton House has been much changed. The entrance hall has a groined vault – doubtless of lath and plaster – and leads to a wide and similarly vaulted cross-corridor, decorated by Ionic pilasters, each with its own piece of full entablature – perhaps an idea from Crichton. The left-hand end of the ground-floor corridor terminates in a fine stairhall, with a cantilevered, dog-leg staircase with cast-iron balusters; this hall was originally side-lit through a Diocletian window – perhaps, again, an idea from Crichton, since such semi-circular tripartite windows were much used in Adam's building for Edinburgh University. The door to the former dining room is at the right-hand end of this corridor. The former drawing room with its shallow bow is in the centre and enjoys the superb view.

Forbes appears to have been annoyed by Harrison's approach – he sent several sketch plans, rather than presentation drawings – but Harrison was equally displeased with Forbes' attitude to his architects and was probably unwilling to spend precious time on what he regarded as perhaps fruitless work. The situation probably arose because professional practice still differed in the two countries. Since Forbes had great influence in Edinburgh, he has been credited with terminating Harrison's career in Scotland – but it has to be said that no English architect has ever built up a continuous practice in Scotland. Why should Harrison have been different? There were good Scots architects a-plenty in 1800, as the New Town in Edinburgh demonstrates beyond doubt.

Harrison's country houses in Scotland can be securely attributed, but there is also a country house near Lancaster, which he almost certainly designed, before he left the town in 1795, that is to say, between Kennet and Broomhall. This is **Quernmore Park Hall**, which was built from 1795 to 1798 for Charles Gibson, who had bought the Quernmore estate in 1793. He was a descendant of a Preston lawyer, who had bought the estate of Myerscough House in 1731 to set his family up as minor gentry. He had inherited land elsewhere in small parcels, but purchase of the 1300-acre Quernmore estate made him a significant landowner. He enclosed the estate during the next few years and soon gained the reputation of being a good progressive farmer. He moved the old road from Lancaster to Caton about half–a-mile to the east, so that his new house could stand in the middle of its undulating landscaped park, looking over the Conder valley.[14] It is not open to the public.

Quernmore Park Hall [Figure 36] is an elegantly austere house, built of pale sandstone ashlar in largish blocks, quarried on the estate. The interior of the house was substantially altered in the 1840s by Alexander Mills for its new owner, William Garnett, but the exterior, apart from the porch, which Mills also designed, is much as originally built.

The format of the house – with its two-and-a-half storey central block, wings and pedimented pavilions with tripartite windows – is that of a major Palladian house. This was somewhat old-fashioned in the mid-1790s, but the austerity of the façade was certainly well up-to-date. Its central block

[Figure 36] Quernmore Park Hall, *c.*2000. Reproduced by permission of the owner.

has five widely spaced windows under a shallow hipped roof. All the windows have plain jambs, and the only decoration is a band at the level of the first-floor windowsills.

Quernmore is fairly rare among Georgian country houses, in that it has only one façade, looking out over the park. Behind the centre of the main block is a two-storey block containing service rooms, and to each side of the main block the pavilions extend to the rear to enclose a service yard – similar to, but larger than, the one at Lytham Hall.

Mills changed the original internal layout significantly, by replacing the large central stairhall with a fine and striking two-storey atrium, and by extending the original subsidiary staircase to become the main one. Harrison's original staircase (which is shown in a plan by Mills) had risen from right to left around the curved side of a semi-circular top-lit hall; it must have looked rather like the spectacular main staircase in the recently built Somerset House, London, leading to the Great Hall, where the Royal Academy held its annual exhibition. (Harrison appears to have designed a similar staircase at Grove House at Allerton – see page 103.) The layout of both main floors, with their rectangular rooms, grouped around the atrium, is, however, still as it was first designed; the fine mahogany doors with planted mouldings must be original too, but most of the cornices and all of the fireplaces are later.

The question of the attribution of Quernmore Park Hall to Harrison is difficult – not least because, with its two-and-a-half storeys, it does not look like his other designs for new houses – but it is not uninteresting. Colvin rightly doubts the traditional attribution to Harrison in Sir Bernard Burke's *Visitations of Seats and Arms*, published in 1852: by that date the house no longer belonged to the builder's family, and it has to be said that later owners of attractive houses have been known to attribute them to famous architects. However, Charles Gibson's grandson, Rev. George Gibson, wrote some 250 pages of *Memorials of the family of Gibson* in 1862 and states clearly on page 161 that the Hall was built 'from a design of Mr Harrison, Architect of Chester'.[15] This is not, of course, conclusive, since it was written nearly 40 years after Charles Gibson's death, but does lend credence to the traditional attribution. Furthermore, there is, in the Grosvenor Museum, Chester, a sketch[(*)] for a presentation drawing [Figure 37], which shows the house almost exactly as built and also has the same inaccuracies of perspective as the drawing at Broomhall [Figure 34], which is mentioned above. In consequence, I believe that Harrison almost certainly designed a house with two storeys and then, presumably at Gibson's request, one with

---

[(*)] It must be only a sketch, because on the back of the paper there is a roughly drawn but accurately dimensioned plan and half-elevation of the house, almost as built. I can think of no other plausible reason for the presence of these drawings in Chester than that they were made by Harrison.

[Figure 37]
Quernmore Park
Hall: Harrison's
drawing for the
proposed Entrance
Front, c.1795.
Reproduced by
permission of the
Grosvenor
Museum, Chester
City Council.

two-and-a-half storeys – the drawings for both are now among the Garnett papers. However, when he had to leave Lancaster, he must have lost the supervision of the building of this second design to another architect, who slightly changed the details of the façade. Who might this have been? The most likely man is John Webb,[16] who laid out the park at Quernmore, and also designed (the slightly later) Leck Hall and Casterton Hall.

The traditional main approach to the Quernmore Park Hall is from the A683, and at this entrance to the estate stands the **Chain Lodge**. It is basically an idiosyncratic re-working of a typical Palladian design, with a two-storey centre and lower side bays. The centre is flanked by giant Tuscan pilasters, which carry a segmental arch and an open pediment above the first-floor window. The front door stands behind two Tuscan columns with a deep plain frieze and a cornice, which is continued above the side bays. Harrison probably designed it with the house.

CHAPTER EIGHT

Buildings in Liverpool and Manchester, 1800–1815

When he had moved to Chester, Harrison must have hoped that he would also receive some commissions in Liverpool and Manchester, which were already the most important towns in the north west. Within a few years those hopes had been fulfilled and had resulted in fine works which are historically significant. It was in Liverpool that Harrison first used an Ionic portico, and in Manchester that he introduced fluted Doric columns.

His work in the two cities started in **Liverpool** when he entered a competition in the summer of 1800 for a building to accommodate both a newsroom and coffee house, and also new premises for the long-established Liverpool Library. The competition was in fact won by John Foster, the Surveyor to the Corporation of Liverpool, but his plan was too expensive for the committee, so they chose to build one of Harrison's alternative designs. The building contract was signed in March 1801, and work was finished by the summer of 1802, at a cost of £11,000.[1]

The Lyceum introduced both the gentlemen's club and Greek motifs to Liverpool. It stands at the lower end of Bold Street, which was by 1800 a fashionable residential address. [Figure 38] The entrance façade of good ashlar appears as a tall single-storey building of three very wide bays – an enlargement of the format of Springfield Hall – but there is also a hidden mezzanine floor, and a basement under the left-hand third. The actual entrances to the library and newsroom are within a recessed Ionic portico with six giant, unfluted columns – not monoliths, but made from three drums. Harrison had planned such a portico outside the Shire Hall at Chester in the mid-1790s, but later made it free-standing. This one in Liverpool may well therefore be the first recessed portico to be built in England. It is flanked by broad tripartite windows, with unfluted Doric columns for mullions, under a segmental relieving arch.

In striking contrast to this relaxed elegance, the side façade to Waterloo Place is more forceful: it has five narrow bays, of which the central three are emphasised by Ionic half-columns, carrying a cornice with an attic, rather than a pediment. Above the three central windows, which lit the newsroom, there are panels, carved with bas-reliefs of Geography, Apollo, and Commerce, to symbolise Liverpool's claims to be England's second

port and a significant cultural centre. Both the main entablature of the Bold Street façade and the cornice within the tripartite windows wrap around the corner, neatly linking the two façades into one design, but the Waterloo Place façade appears taller, especially now that the space in front of the basement has been opened up.

[Figure 38]
Liverpool: The
Lyceum, 2004.

The Lyceum was the object of a *cause célèbre* of conservation planning in the 1970s: it escaped demolition, but is no longer used for its original purposes. Much of its original layout and a few of its original fittings and decorations can, however, be seen. (Joseph Farington visited the building on 22 September 1808 and was impressed enough with it to draw a sketch plan in his diary.) The central doorway within the portico leads straight on to the original Library, which is now a bar. It is a circular space, about 50 feet in diameter, under a top-lit dome, which hangs from the main roof timbers. Within it stands a circle of twelve reeded Tuscan columns, which carry a gallery, originally lined with bookcases – a traditional format. [Figure 39] The dome, which rises above the gallery level, is a panelled hemi-sphere. Historians have sought ingeniously for precedents for this domed library, but I surmise that Harrison's basic inspiration came simply from his memories of the Pantheon.

The left-hand door within the portico leads to the former Newsroom and Coffee Room. It is a fine, light space, measuring about 70 feet by 50, with a segmental ceiling, which rises to some 20 feet. It has a deep fireplace recess on the side wall, whose junction with the main space is now marked

by a cluster of Ionic columns, which cannot be original. The frieze above the windows is decorated with painted panels, showing battles and processions; it is unlikely that Harrison designed them, but their overtones of the Elgin Marbles would probably have appealed to him.

The first of Harrison's buildings in **Manchester,** and the only survivor, is another gentlemen's newsroom and library, the **Portico Library** on Mosley Street. It was designed in 1802 for men who been impressed by the Lyceum, and there are similarities between the two buildings – not least because the Library is also the building with which Harrison introduced Greek details into Manchester. It was begun in the summer of 1803, built at a cost of some £6,800, and opened in January 1806. It is built of brick, but faced with large blocks of ashlar. It stands on the corner of Mosley Street and Charlotte Street, on a site which in 1802 belonged to a man called Peter Marsland, who first leased it and then sold it to the Library. It has therefore two façades, which have different but, of course, related treatments, as at the Lyceum. [Figure 40]

The entrance façade on Mosley Street looks – as it was meant to – like a little temple, with a recessed portico with four giant Ionic columns, formed of three drums and carrying a pediment; its entablature continues round the corner to the seven-bay façade on Charlotte Street. This has a slightly projecting centre, with six giant Ionic half-columns which carry an attic; the lower windows light what was originally the Newsroom and is now a public house.

It is now, sadly, impossible to recapture the three-dimensional quality of the Library's original interior, which can only be seen in an old photograph. [Figure 41] The whole room was tall and spacious – about 60 feet long, by some 40 feet wide and high – and open to the ceiling of what is now the upper room; it was lit from above and by the windows on Charlotte Street.

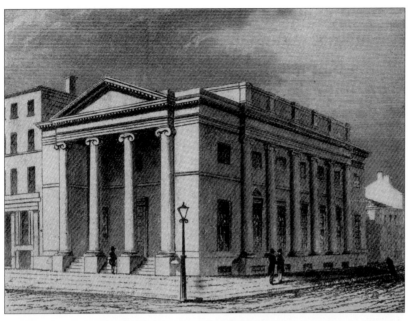

[Figure 40]
Left: Manchester:
The Portico
Library, *c.*1825.

[Figure 41]
Below: Manchester:
The original
interior of the
Portico Library,
*c.*1910. Reproduced
by permission of
the Portico Library.

The original ground floor was used as the Newsroom, with the Library's bookcases – much as in the Lyceum – on an upper gallery, supported on cast-iron Doric columns, which contained pipes for a somewhat ineffective central heating system.[2] (A ceiling, supported on two rows of paired Roman Doric columns, was inserted in 1921 at the level of this gallery, to create a bank, now the pub, on the ground floor.)

The floor of the present upper storey is at the level of the gallery. The Library, with its fitted bookcases on all four sides, is still preserved and still in use. It is a beautifully serene space under a top-lit saucer dome, hung from the roof timbers; this may have been inspired by some of Soane's (now demolished) interiors in the Bank of England and rises some 20 feet between wide segmental arches. The whole space must, however, appear more serene now than it did before 1921, because it is only about half as high – since one cannot see the ground floor through the central space. The architect, Thomas Rickman, was very impressed with the library in its original form, when he saw it on 23 August 1817, confiding to his diary that it was 'the best interior I have seen of Harrison's'. It is, therefore, fitting that, as well as portrait medallions of Shakespeare and Milton, a bust of Harrison, in the distinguished guise of a Roman gentleman, can be seen in the room. [See page 136.]

Harrison's second building in *Manchester* was the *Theatre Royal*, which was built in 1806 and opened in 1807, at a cost of about £12,000. It was a large building, standing on the corner of Fountain Street and Charlotte Street with a spacious stage and seats for 1,020 people. It was destroyed by fire in 1844. Contemporary descriptions[3] suggest that it was undistinguished – unsurprisingly, since Georgian theatres enjoyed no public subsidies and tended to be built cheaply.

Harrison's third commission in *Manchester* has also disappeared. This was the *Exchange*, an imposing meeting place for merchants, who were not ashamed of their wealth, nor of its source in trade. It replaced an earlier Exchange and provided members with a newsroom, library and dining room, and also a post-office. It stood on the corner of Market Street and Exchange Street – on the north-western quarter of the present Royal Exchange.[(*)] Harrison had produced his first plans in February 1805 but, presumably because of the pressure of other work, was not able to produce the final plans for a year. The contract was signed in the sum of £12,320; the foundation stone was laid in July 1806, and the building was opened in January 1809.

As at the Portico Library, the structure was of brick, faced with ashlar on the main façades. Contemporary illustrations show that it played an

---

[(*)] As the membership of the Exchange grew, Harrison's building was enlarged in 1849 and then replaced in 1874; this replacement was itself superseded by the present Royal Exchange in 1921.

impressive part in the streetscape. [Figure 42] Its façades were dominated by giant, fluted, Doric half-columns, carrying a triglyph frieze. This was Harrison's first use of the Doric columns with fluted shafts – preceding the Propylaea Gateway at Chester Castle by a couple of years. The entrance on Market Street was set in a semi-circular front with nine bays. Inside, behind this façade, the plan and section of the spacious, semi-circular news-room would have been interesting: the room was lit by a glazed semi-dome and was surrounded by a gallery, carried on fluted Ionic columns; this was used by a circulating library – a scheme doubtless derived from the Lyceum in Liverpool.

Liverpool is the home of the only one of Harrison's church buildings, which is a significant structure and which remains much as he left it – **the tower of the Church of Our Lady and St Nicholas**, on Chapel Street. [Figure 43] The spire on the medieval tower had collapsed in February 1810, destroying the tower and killing about 20 worshippers. Harrison was asked to design a replacement – probably because Liverpool was then in the Diocese of Chester. His plans were accepted in September 1810, the foundation stone was laid in 1811, and work was finished in 1815, at a cost of something over £22,000.

It is without doubt his best work at a church and, fortunately, survived the Blitz in 1940. Built of ashlar, it rises to a height of 120 feet in three stages between the vestries at the west end of the church. Its upper windows have ogee-arched hoodmoulds, rather like those on the tower of Chester Cathedral. The buttresses at the corners project above the battlemented parapet as octagonal pinnacles and abut tiny flying buttresses, which support the octagonal open-work spire. This was a pleasing addition to the original design, made in 1814, and is reminiscent

[Figure 42] Manchester: The Exchange, 1817. Reproduced by permission of Manchester Archives and Local Studies.

[Figure 43]
Liverpool: George Cuitt's etching of St Nicholas' steeple,
1816. Reproduced by permission of the Grosvenor
Museum, Chester City Council.

of the lantern of some York churches –
for example, All Saints, Pavement –
which Harrison must have seen, when
he went there in 1810 to advise on the
rebuilding of the Ouse Bridge (see
Appendix B). It looks almost medieval,
but that was not Harrison's aim. As in
his other Gothick works, he did not
want to copy the motifs of a past age to
create a counterfeit, but simply to
produce a courteous design which
might also hint at the longevity of
Liverpool.

Harrison also designed a saucer-
domed ceiling to improve the acoustics
of the now-demolished St Paul's church
in Liverpool in 1818, but St Nicholas'
church was his last significant work
there. After 1815 major building work in
and around Liverpool and Manchester
was entrusted increasingly to local
architects – like the younger John
Foster and Richard Lane respectively –
who produced designs of high quality
and often in the fashionable Grecian
manner, which Harrison had
introduced. This must have been rather
galling for him, but he celebrated his
60th birthday in 1804 and probably
accepted the situation with equanimity.
Thereafter the bulk of his work was
carried out on secular buildings in
Chester or within 20 miles or so of that
city. However, before describing them,
it is appropriate to look briefly at his
other churches.

CHAPTER NINE

Churches, 1802–19

'Briefly' is the appropriate word, since Harrison designed very few churches, and – with the exception of the tower and spire at St Nicholas' in Liverpool – none is a significant work.

His first church commission was at **Whittington**, in Shropshire. The medieval **Church of St John the Baptist** had been badly damaged in a storm, and Harrison was asked by the Rector, the Rev W.W. Davies (who had lived as a young man at Broughton Hall, just south-west of Chester) to design a new and wider nave, between the existing west tower and chancel. The faculty, which was granted in October 1802, contains an unsigned plan, which corresponds closely to the existing building.[1] Work began in 1805 and was finished, at a cost of about £1,500, in 1806. One can still see the basic shape of Harrison's three-bay, brick-built nave with its pedimented gables and its plain round-headed windows, recessed under shallow arches. However, most of the details in and out have been replaced by later 'improvements', of which the most obvious is the elaborate terracotta tracery, placed in 1894 within the windows.

There was no need for new Anglican churches in **Chester** – there were already nine parish churches in addition to the cathedral – so Harrison's first work there was the simple matter of re-facing in red sandstone the south side of **St Peter's Church,** which stands by the Cross in the centre of the city. A two-storey timber-framed lean-to, built to accommodate the Mayor's office and also the Rector's house, had stood against that side of the church for 300 years before it was pulled down in 1803, so that the road could be widened. Harrison's task in 1804 was merely to tidy the appearance of the church. [Figure 44] He was also asked in 1813 to reface the tower, and the two-light tracery in the bell-openings is probably to his design, but his nave windows with their intersecting tracery were replaced in 1886 by the present ones, designed by John Douglas.

His third church – the **Methodist Church** in **Chester** – suffered much the same fate as his first. Its three-bay shell was built in dark-brown bricks to Harrison's designs in 1811 – a rainwater hopper on the south-western corner bears that date – but the specification for the internal works, including a gallery, was provided by the main contractor William Cole. The fashionably bowed two-storey front to St John's Street was replaced in 1906 with a typical – and not unattractive – red-brick entrance façade with

[Figure 44]
Chester: St Peter's
church, as refaced
by Harrison, *c*.1820.

a large nine-light window, filled with Perpendicular tracery. At the same
time the interior was also significantly changed.

Harrison's fourth church has also suffered greatly from later alterations,
to the extent of being unrecognisable. It was built between 1814 and 1816 as
the *Chapel of West Hall, High Legh,* near Lymm, but is now the Church
of St John at High Legh. The owner of West Hall, Egerton Legh, wanted
to replace a ruinous chapel of 1408 and also celebrate the coming of peace
in Europe. The chapel was a simple four-bay building with a gabled west
front, decorated with four Ionic half-columns. It was burnt out in 1891,
after which the lowest courses of its walls were incorporated into a new
parish church with applied timber framing and a spire.

St Nicholas' Church in Liverpool is probably the only one of his church
commissions, which gave Harrison much satisfaction. He may have hoped
for a similar outcome in July 1818, when the Bishop, Dr George Law,
launched an appeal for repairs to **Chester Cathedral** and asked him to carry
out the work. The main problem was in the **south transept**, where the
stability of the south wall was giving concern, but work was also necessary
on the tracery of most of the windows and on some of the gutters. Harrison
wrote a memorandum on the necessary repairs in February 1819, produced
a number of drawings[3] and expected, after the approval of his plans, to
supervise the work. However, he was disagreeably surprised, when it became
clear that the Dean, who – rather than the Bishop – was responsible for the
maintenance of the cathedral fabric, wanted to employ the craftsmen whom
Harrison had chosen, but to pay someone else to supervise the
implementation of his plans.

Harrison responded with some asperity in a letter to the Chapter

Clerk, claiming that he had examined the cathedral and 'made the necessary drawings, specifications and estimates etc, preparatory to commencing the operations'. He continued that he 'presumed that the Dean … wished to have a professional man of some experience to advise with, and to superintend the necessary works of this decayed building', and then asked rhetorically, 'You cannot imagine that I, or any other person, would willingly lend his name as architect to the repairs required in this almost ruinous church[*] … without having the superintendence of such repairs…. Would the public be as ready to free me from the responsibility of any failure, as the Chapter express themselves to be? I doubt it much.'[4]

His argument was not just that he was going to lose fee income, but that, since he had designed the works, it was only sensible for him to supervise them, to ensure that they were carried out properly, in the interests of the client and of the architect's reputation. This was the normal practice by then in England, but Harrison was politely asked not go onto the site any more.

This sorry little story shows not so much a clash of personalities – though that may have played a part – as a conflict of cultures. Harrison had seen this in Scotland and suggested that the Dean and Chapter might be 'not well acquainted with the usual mode of conducting work of this nature'. He may well have been right that the Chapter really did not know how work was done in 1819 in the secular world. It is quite possible that their attitudes were still those of the medieval Chapter, which would have appointed one of their number as 'guardian of the works' and regarded him as responsible both for obtaining the designs, and for supervising the craftsmen who carried them out.

The work of building Harrison's deep buttresses at the south end of the south transept, designed to withstand the thrust of the arcades inside, went ahead. [Figure 45] Their flat tops are decorated with simple arched niches and minimal battlements, but, without pinnacles and prominent offsets, they do not look medieval and are now edited out of all the standard images of the cathedral. The work on the transept's gutters, recommended by Harrison, but done without his supervision, was badly done and needed repairs again in 1826.

It may seem strange that, when Harrison and most of his colleagues were designing in the Classical manner, they were at pains to use motifs, for which they could cite an appropriate Greek or Roman precedent, but were not so painstaking when it came to designing work in a medieval context. The reason for this apparent inconsistency is that the study of medieval building styles had not progressed so far by 1820 as that of Classical

[*] Harrison's language was forthright, but his opinion was probably valid, since virtually no repair works had been carried out at the cathedral since the 1530s.

[Figure 45]
Chester Cathedral,
showing, on the far
left, Harrison's new
buttresses on the
façade of the South
Transept, *c.*1820.

architecture by 1750. By 1840 the medievalists had caught up, but that is
another story.

Harrison was not paid his fee of £25 for his drawings until after his death
ten years later, and then only when his executors asked. In Harrison's eyes
he was a professional man, entitled to fairly prompt payment for services
rendered, but to the Dean he was no more than a superior tradesman, whose
bills could be paid when it was convenient. It is probably not unfair to
suggest that there may also have been another dimension to the Dean's
conduct, that he may well have remembered the controversy in 1808 over
the Northgate in Chester (see page 93) when he had been ranged with the
City's Tory MP, Lord Egerton, against Lord Grosvenor, the Whig MP,
who favoured Harrison's design. Chester was not a million miles from
Barsetshire.

CHAPTER TEN

Later Works, 1801–15

Thomas Harrison 'of Chester' deserves his nickname. For the last 30 years of his life the bulk of his commissions came from public bodies or private citizens in Chester, or within 20 miles or so of that city, in Cheshire or in the neighbouring counties of North Wales.

In their variety but also their inter-relatedness, these buildings are typical of a non-specialist architect's practice at that time and, indeed, now. It is, however, appropriate to divide the story into two chapters, with a break in 1815, since that was the year in which work on the great Propylaea Gateway to Chester Castle was finished, and in which also Harrison designed the last of his houses using motifs from ancient Greece. Thereafter his work was typical of the age in deriving its decorative motifs both from the traditional Classical repertoire and from the increasingly fashionable Middle Ages.

Harrison's first two commissions in this period were for public buildings, but both have disappeared. The first came from the County JPs in 1801 and involved repairs to the *House of Correction* at *Middlewich*. This stood on Queen Street, and was demolished in the second half of the nineteenth century. The second commission came in 1806 – probably as a result of his work at Middlewich – and was to design a new *City Gaol and House of Correction* in *Chester*, to replace the one which had stood for centuries within the Northgate. The complex was built of brick between 1806 and 1808, at a cost of some £3,500, on what is now the site of the Queen's School on City Walls Road. It comprised a gaol in the western half (for people awaiting trial) and a house of correction on the east (for those found guilty of a misdemeanour). Each prison building was shaped like a cross, with a square courtyard within each angle. Everything was surrounded by a high wall, with two separate entrances, each with its stone porch on four Doric columns.

Harrison's next work fortunately survives – the **Commercial News Room**, which stands just to the north of St Peter's church, on Northgate Street in **Chester**. It was designed in 1807 for a group of men, who had decided that Chester, like Liverpool and Manchester, needed a place where gentlemen could read newspapers in the comfort of a club. It is now the home of the Chester City Club and not open to the public.[1]

The site is deep but narrow and originally accommodated on the front a public house and a couple of small shops. Ownership of the site was shared by the City Council and Lord Grosvenor, but they were prepared to sell it for a more genteel purpose. The unpretentious but decent 'Commercial Inn' was built to Harrison's designs in 1807 on the rear of the site. The News Room, which cost some £2,700, was opened in January 1808.

The building has an elegant two-storey, three-bay façade of sandstone ashlar. The tall first-floor windows, placed between unfluted monolithic Ionic half-columns, which carry a pediment, light the former News Room. The panel above the central window is carved with an anchor and a military standard crossed – to suggest news of battles at sea and on land. The ground floor has been significantly changed since 1808: the three segmental arches and rusticated piers date from 1923, and the walkway behind them dates from 1962. Under Harrison's scheme, which can be seen on an old invoice [Figure 46], the ground floor had plain piers and three round-headed arches, the central one leading to an entrance lobby for a pair of shops, whose windows stood directly behind the outer arches. The entrance to the stairs to the News Room is at the back, and the News Room itself (now used as a billiards room) is a fine space, about 20 feet high and measuring some 40 feet by 25. It has an apsidal end to the north and a shallow segmental ceiling, decorated with simple panels.

Harrison made a number of designs for Lowther Hall in Westmorland in 1804, but the work was abortive (see Appendix B), so his first commission at a gentleman's seat since designing Colinton House was carried out between 1807 and 1811 for Lord Kenyon at *Gredington* in Flintshire.[2] Kenyon was a lawyer, whom Harrison had known since 1787, when the Cheshire magistrates were seeking an Act of Parliament to allow the rebuilding of Chester Castle. The work at Gredington involved enlarging and remodelling the rear of an older house, at a cost of £6,675. The middle

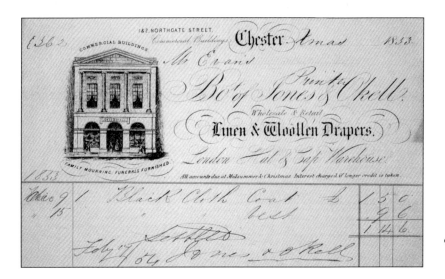

[Figure 46]
Chester:
Commercial
Newsroom, as
originally designed,
1853.

three bays of the garden front were emphasised – somewhat as at Broomhall – by pairs of Ionic columns on the ground floor and pilaster strips above. The house was demolished in 1978.

Harrison's next work was for a public client, the City of **Chester**. Three of the City's four medieval gates had been replaced in the later eighteenth century. The first had been the Eastgate, built in 1769; then had come the Bridgegate in 1782 and the Watergate in 1789, both designed by Joseph Turner. All three are elegant structures, built to carry the walkway of the walls – by then a fashionable promenade – over the roads to the city centre. The building of a new **Northgate**, after the removal of the city gaol, was the idea of Earl Grosvenor, who had been elected Mayor in 1807. The suggestion was accepted in principle by the City Council's Assembly Committee in January 1808, but thereafter the complicated story of the design and building of the Northgate – it is told in detail in Ockrim[3] – is hardly edifying; it is a web of parish-pump politics, from which no-one comes out well.

Grosvenor wanted a Gothick design for a gate in the largely medieval walls of the City, so Harrison produced a pretty confection with a parapet of arches carrying a vaulted passage over the road.[4] However, he pointed out to Grosvenor that the new gate would stand on the site of a Roman gate, within a few yards of an impressive stretch of the surviving Roman wall. He then persuaded Grosvenor of the merits of his own preferred design – which, with its columns, harked back to Chester's foundation in Roman times. When the Committee discussed the matter again on 20 May 1808, Harrison presented his new plans, but, when the vote was taken, only two members supported him, while ten voted for building a copy of Joseph Turner's elegant Watergate. A Mr Anderson, who was supplying Runcorn stone for the work on the Castle and whom Harrison had recommended as the builder of the new gate, said he could build Turner's design for £280, rather than the £350 which Harrison estimated as the cost of his design. Money was, as always, an important consideration, but there are also dark hints in the Minutes and in the ensuing public controversy that some people regarded Harrison as a pushing outsider. There was also some national political in-fighting behind the scenes, which set supporters of the recently elected Tory MP – who included the Dean of the Cathedral – against Earl Grosvenor's brother, the City's other MP, who was a Whig.

Within a fortnight Anderson had excavated for the foundations of Turner's design, but strong opposition was already being expressed in the city to the idea of a copy of an old-fashioned gate, when an up-to-date design was on offer. Grosvenor's faction, who were willing to pay the higher price, were eventually successful, and Anderson built the new gateway to Harrison's design. This was in fact modified a little, while it was being built, becoming more severe in appearance and gaining more of the 'noble simplicity and quiet grandeur' of the Shire Hall portico. [Figure 47]

The Northgate is built of large blocks of ashlar, 18 inches deep. The arch over the road is segmental, and its underside is divided into four coffered sections by five monolithic voussoirs, spanning from front to back of the structure, which is eight feet thick. The tall openings for the pavements are framed, on both faces of the gate, by pairs of monolithic Doric half-columns. Harrison had wanted fluted columns, on the grounds that they were more authentically Greek, but was persuaded to drop the idea by the Town Clerk, who feared that the flutings would be damaged by the mob 'at a time of disputed elections'. These columns support an entablature with a plain frieze, whose cornice runs from side to side of the structure and carries a plain parapet, bearing a Latin inscription. The one on the inner face gives the names of the mayors and also of the architect – an honour indeed for Harrison.

Charles Cockerell saw the Northgate in 1823 and wrote in his diary that it was 'an excellent work, the effect chiefly arising from the admirable constructive style of the masonry, in particular the arches'.[5] This must mean that he was impressed by Harrison's appreciation of the importance of structure, as distinct from decoration, in architecture, which is shown by the way in which the voussoirs and coffers make clear how the central arch is built.

Harrison's first work for a Cheshire gentleman was the creation of a **picture gallery** between 1808 and 1810 for Sir John Fleming Leicester, at **Tabley House**. Leicester was a major collector of Old Masters and one of the most important patrons of contemporary British artists, and his was

[Figure 47]
Chester: Northgate, 1815. Reproduced by permission of the Grosvenor Museum, Chester City Council.

one of the first private picture galleries. Tabley House, which was built in the 1760s to the designs of John Carr, is open to the public.

To create the gallery, Harrison combined three west-facing rooms on the main floor. Since there would be more windows in the south wall of the new room than in the north, he had to block them all and lower the sills of the western windows. The main structural work was to replace two internal load-bearing walls with shallow segmental arches, similar to those in the Portico Library and Chester's Northgate, thus creating a fine but fairly low tripartite space, which measures about 70 feet by 30 and has a central bay window. What we see now, however, is not quite what Harrison designed. A lithograph of the Picture Gallery [Figure 48], which can be seen in the room itself and must date from before 1826, shows that Harrison's treatment of the arches was simpler than what is there today – with no more than simple flutings on the pilasters and a guilloche motif on the arches themselves. The present rich plasterwork and the low bookcases are thought to date from the 1840s.[6]

Harrison's next work was for a public client at **Denbigh**, where he designed the **Denbighshire Infirmary** on Ruthin Road. This had been founded by the Rector of Denbigh in 1807 as a Dispensary 'for the relief of the sick and diseased poor'. Since it was the first of its kind in North Wales, its facilities were soon overloaded, and a subscription was started to raise the money for building special premises. A local guidebook, published in 1829,[7] relates that the designs were given by Harrison in 1810, and that the building was finished early in 1813.

The Infirmary has been extended several times, but the T-shaped heart of the present building, with its bricks, laid in Flemish bond, is the two-storey,

[Figure 48] Tabley House: Picture Gallery, c.1825. Reproduced by permission of Tabley House and the University of Manchester

seven-bay building illustrated in the guide-book. The central bay, which contained a pedimented porch, carried on two Tuscan columns, was the only hint of Classical design. Hubbard found it hard to believe that this 'rather uninspired' building could be by Harrison,[8] but a local historian in 1856 called it 'plain but handsome'.[9] I surmise that Harrison had simply been asked to design something decent but cheap, and easy to build without his supervision.

Denbigh Infirmary was in fact Harrison's last design for a building in the public domain – apart from some internal alterations in around 1820 to the *Exchange* in *Chester* (which was burnt down in 1862). Thereafter all his works were private houses, plus some monuments and bridges.

It was probably about the time that he was working on the Infirmary at Denbigh, that he was commissioned to design a house, called **Oughtrington Hall,** near Lymm. [Figure 49] Ormerod stated in 1819 that the house had been built recently for Mr Trafford Trafford, a Cheshire JP who had inherited the house in 1806 on the death of John Legh.[10] There is some doubt about the attribution to Harrison, but this is due largely to the ambiguity of a documentary source,[(*)] and I believe, on the evidence of the

[Figure 49]
Oughtrington Hall:
Entrance Façade,
2004.

(*) J. H. Hanshall in his *History of the County Palatine of Chester* (1817) stated that the house had been built 'after a design by Mr Harrison', but he called it the Lodge – which has led people astray. The actual gate-lodge on Oughtrington Lane was probably designed by Harrison along with the big house; it has a porch carried on two Tuscan columns between pilasters.

house itself, that Harrison almost certainly designed it. It was extended after 1862 and again in the 1920s, and now forms a small part of a large secondary school, which is not open to the general public.

The house stands on the top of a hill with extensive views eastwards over the Mersey valley to the Pennines. It appears to have been built originally of brick with a stone sill-band on the first floor and a stone cornice, but is now rendered and lined to give 12-inch 'courses'. The east-facing entrance façade has two storeys (above cellars) and three wide bays, with a semi-octagonal centre. This is a new motif in Harrison's work and might be a version of the canted bay windows which Carr had used at Tabley House. The main windows on both floors originally had 12-pane sashes. To each side of the centre there is, on the ground floor, a tripartite window, with Tuscan colonnettes, under a segmental relieving arch. The porch, which also creates a balcony for what was probably the main bedroom, extends in front of the centre and follows its plan. It is carried on two pairs of tall monolithic Tuscan columns at the front corners and on a single column to the sides, but the height of these columns means – unfortunately – that their cornice does not line up with the cornice in the windows, and that the first floor appears somewhat low.

The interior suggests that Harrison did little more than re-front an older house: the mahogany doors with their planted mouldings could well be by him, but the fine fireplaces with their fluted sidepieces and carved mantelshelves in the rooms to the left of the entrance probably date from the 1770s. Furthermore, the spacious open-well staircase with three turned balusters per tread and a ramped handrail must date from before 1750; Trafford probably regarded it as too good to lose.

At much the same time as Harrison was working on Oughtrington Hall, he was also designing an ambitious suburban villa – **Woodbank**, which now stands in a large public park on the edge of **Stockport**. [Figure 50] The house was built between 1812 and 1814 for Peter Marsland,[11] who had been the owner of the site, on which the Portico Library in Manchester now stands. He was the owner of a large cotton-spinning mill in Stockport, and his house there was attacked in 1812 by Luddite machine-breakers. He therefore had this new house built, a mile out of the town, on the edge of a steep slope above a picturesque loop in the River Goyt, with a good view to the Pennines. The attribution to Harrison only dates from 1850, but must be almost certain, because the house was then lived in by the builder's son and bears many of Harrison's hallmarks. It is now used as offices and is not open to the public.

The house is a large, two-storey villa, built of large blocks of the local sandstone, under a shallow hipped roof. The entrance façade, on the south, has three very wide bays and a segmental porch, carried on four monolithic Ionic columns, about 11 feet tall. The tripartite windows on either side are slightly recessed under a segmental arch; their mullions are square with sunk

panels. Dimensions and most details are similar to those at Springfield Hall, except that the first-floor windows – because of the tall columns on the ground floor – are low, with only nine-pane sashes. Harrison's obvious pleasure in tall monolithic columns led him astray here, as at Oughtrington, but more so: the upper floor lacks vertical emphasis, which spoils the appearance of the whole façade.

[Figure 50]
Woodbank,
Entrance Façade,
2004.

The cornice of the porch continues around to the east façade and divides it into two storeys. This façade still has three wide bays, but they are treated in a way which offsets the relatively low height of the first floor and gives the façade more vertical emphasis and, therefore, better proportions. [Figure 51] On the bedroom floor, above each pair of Ionic half-columns on the ground floor, there are slight projections with sunk panels – more or less a repeat of the west front of Gredington. The rear façade (on the north) is different again, but is designed to be seen with the east front in one diagonal view. It is flat but has five tall windows and six Ionic half-columns along the ground floor. The fact that there are also five windows on the upper floor gives it a greater vertical emphasis, which counteracts the width of the façade.

The service wing is attached to the west, but the inevitable asymmetry is carefully composed: the service wing's three-bay front echoes that of the house, but its proportions are better and it is discretely set back. Its entrance door is at the back – so that the family and the lower servants need never meet. Several of the rooms in the basement of the house and the service

[Figure 51]
Woodbank: East
and North Façades,
2004.

wing have brick vaults, and a few have arches, supported by wrought-iron beams, as in a contemporary 'fireproof' mill.

Inside, the spacious entrance hall has a panelled ceiling, segmental in profile, which spans from back to front of the space. Like several other rooms in the house it is decorated with probably contemporary plaster relief-panels (brought here, though, in 1930). As in most rooms of the house, the doors are of mahogany, and set in architraves with sunk panels. A door opposite the entrance leads to the slightly smaller, top-lit stair-hall, which contains a wide and shallow staircase with an elegant iron balustrade, cantilevered around an open well. The main rooms enjoy the view.

Another house, where the date and an attribution to Harrison are in some doubt, is **Glan-yr-Afon**, near **Loggerheads** in Denbighshire. [Figure 52] There is no documentary proof of Harrison's involvement, but, since the house has similarities with Oughtrington Hall and since Harrison certainly designed Watergate House in Chester in 1820 for the owner of Glan-yr-Afon, I am inclined to believe that the attribution is probably correct, and that a date of about 1812 – that is, after Oughtrington and Woodbank – is reasonable.

The client was Henry Potts, a prominent solicitor in Chester who was in 1815 to succeed his father, Charles Potts, as Clerk of the Peace in Cheshire – the equivalent of the chief executive of a modern County Council. Charles Potts had also been the clerk and treasurer of the committee responsible for the building work at Chester Castle, and Harrison had known them, father and son, for years. The family had been buying land in the Loggerheads

[Figure 52]
Glan-yr-Afon:
Entrance Front,
2004.

area for decades,[12] so the house was probably built to set the seal on the family's rise into the minor gentry. It is still in private ownership and not open to the public.

It sits in the shallow valley of the River Alyn, with views both upstream and down. It was extended in about 1890, but the older part appears as a typical early-nineteenth-century suburban villa, with a low-pitched hipped roof and projecting eaves. It is now rough-cast, but was probably built of brick – there are brick-vaulted cellars under the whole house – and then rendered with the fashionable stucco. The five-bay entrance front has a wide three-bay centre, which projects slightly as a semi-octagonal bay and creates a better-proportioned façade than at Oughtrington. Its porch is flat-fronted, with two pairs of unfluted Doric columns, and it is flanked by tripartite windows without segmental arches – an improvement, in my view. However, whereas the ground-floor windows have 12-pane sashes, those on the first floor still have only nine panes.

The interior has been much altered, and the entrance hall fills the whole of the centre. The central room at the back was probably the drawing room, but has been reduced to make space for a new staircase. However, most ceilings have their original simple cornices, decorated with a guilloche motif or bundles of reeds, and the architraves of most of the doors and windows are reeded with stylised flowers in the top corners.

At the same time as he was supervising the building of Woodbank, Harrison was also working on **Dee Hills** – now **Old Government House** – in Dee Hills Park, **Chester,** which is the first of the three private houses

[Figure 53]
Chester: Dee Hills,
1831.

he designed in the city. [Figure 53] According to Joseph Hemingway,[13] who was a friend of both architect and client, it was built in 1814 for Robert Baxter.(*) It is now used as private offices and is not open to the public.

It is now rendered and marked with 18-inch 'courses' to look like ashlar, but Hemingway says that it was built of stone. It has two storeys, above extensive, brick-vaulted cellars, and three wide bays on each façade. (The five-bay wing on the left side of the front door is not original.) All the windows have plain jambs with, once more, 12-pane sashes on the ground floor and nine panes on the first. The porch, with its *Roman* Doric columns, is probably not original, since it does not appear on the engraving in Hemingway's book. What is more, the fashionably bowed centre on the adjoining garden front, to the south, is fronted by a semi-circular Ionic colonnade; its four tall columns support a cast-iron balcony on the first floor – so placed, clearly, to enjoy a good view up the Dee valley to the hills.

The main rooms on the ground floor face the view and retain their original generous proportions, but few original decorative features survive. The narrow entrance hall has a segmental ceiling, and the guilloche frieze of its cornice is probably original. The same detail is in the top-lit stairhall, which is immediately behind, but the present dog-leg staircase must date from the late-nineteenth century.

Harrison's next house was again built so that the reception rooms enjoy a fine view – across the Mersey towards the Clwydian Hills. It stands on the top of a low hill in open farmland – now a golf-course – at **Allerton**. The house was named Obelisk House on a map of 1816, doubtless after the nearby eighteenth-century obelisk, raised to terminate a view along an avenue from Allerton Hall; however, since about 1825, it has been known

---

(*) Robert Baxter was probably the attorney of that name, who (according to the *Chester Guide and Directory* of 1795) lived in Foregate Street.

as **Grove House**.[14] It was the first and, probably, the most distinguished of the large suburban villas, laid out in large parks for Liverpool merchants in the early 1800s. Harrison is said to have designed it in 1815 for Jacob Fletcher, a Liverpool merchant.[15] The attribution only dates from 1911 and cannot therefore be regarded as sure, but since no-one has ever doubted it and the house contains a number of Harrison hallmarks, I regard it as almost certain.

The house was used as the clubhouse for the golf course, until it was gutted by fire in November 1944; its ground-floor walls are now a stabilised ruin. The house was built of brick, but faced in a buff-coloured sandstone ashlar with stones 18 inches high; originally it had two storeys of roughly equal height, each with 12-pane sash windows. A photograph, published in 1955,[16] shows that towards the rear the house was built across the contours and had a basement.

The garden front [Figure 54], which faces west, has a fashionably shallow central bow, marked by four widely-spaced, fluted Doric half-columns – monoliths about 11 feet tall; their frieze has three triglyphs between each column. The tripartite windows on either side of the bow have simple square mullions, but do not stand under a segmental relieving arch.

The most striking feature of the house – which was designed to be seen together with the garden front – is its seven-bay, south-facing entrance front, which has a deep colonnade of eight widely spaced, monolithic, stop-fluted Doric columns, carrying a 'triple-triglyph' entablature. The 'ceilings'

[Figure 54]
Allerton: Grove House – Garden Front and Entrance Front, 2004.

of each bay of the colonnade are each made from four stones, measuring about eight feet by two, which are carved to form deep coffers – another indication of Harrison's liking for massive masonry. The extent to which Harrison was able to persuade his clients into paying for expensive displays of Classical columns is striking; it suggests that he was able to flatter their pride and ambitions, as newly rich men, to appear as cultivated and wealthy gentlemen.

A plan in the National Monuments Record, which is printed in Ockrim,[17] shows that the house had a semi-circular staircase, as at Quernmore Park Hall, but nothing now remains of the interior decoration at Allerton, so that we cannot know to what extent – if any – it was inspired by Greek motifs. Complete consistency between exterior and interior design was rare – the best-known example is the slightly earlier Belsay House in Northumberland – and most early-nineteenth-century houses had fashionably up-to-date interiors, even if they were made to look like Greek temples outside. Charles Cockerell remarked on the incongruity of this arrangement at Grange Park, Hampshire, in his diary on 21 January 1823.[18]

The lodge to the house still stands on Allerton Road and is a single-storey, rectangular box under a pyramidal roof with a central chimney stack. It has a portico with two pairs of stop-fluted Doric columns, carrying an entablature, which continues, with widely spaced triglyphs, around the whole building.

Although Harrison introduced Doric porticos in plans for a palace in the Ukraine in 1823 (see Appendix B), Grove House was the last of his private houses, inspired by Greek examples. However, he did use Greek motifs in a number of the monuments, which he was commissioned to design between 1810 and 1820, and so it is appropriate to look at them next, before dealing with his last houses.

CHAPTER ELEVEN

Monuments, 1810–24

The impact of the wars against France in the early 1800s has been mentioned more than once. The relief, and the rejoicing, were all the greater, when at last in 1815 Napoleon was beaten at Waterloo. The defeat of Napoleon was not, however, the only reason to build a monument during Harrison's lifetime. The hilltops and parklands of England are peppered with monuments to this or that – for example the obelisk on Castle Howe, Kendal, raised in 1788 to celebrate the centenary of the 'Glorious Revolution', or the column to commemorate Sir Rowland Hill, the first Anglican Lord Mayor of London, at Hawkstone in 1795. Late-Georgian architects doodled monuments in idle moments or spent many hours to produce enticing drawings as testimonies to their imagination and skill, and Harrison was no exception. Few large monuments were built, however, since they cost money, tend to lose their significance within a few years, but need maintenance in perpetuity.

The first stimulus for Harrison to produce the design of a monument, which could actually be built, was the Golden Jubilee of George III in 1810. The King was then sliding into the mental illness, which in the next year allowed his son to become Prince Regent, but his popularity was growing, probably because he was a symbol of national resistance to Napoleon. Harrison, on his own initiative, proposed a column with a 40-foot monolithic shaft at Chester, but nothing came of this suggestion.

However, the idea of a *Jubilee Tower* on **Moel Fammau**, the summit of the Clwydian Range, was mooted in January 1810 by Rev W. W. Davies, the former rector of Whittington and the owner of Llanerch Hall, near St Asaph, from which one can clearly see the mountain. He wrote to Lord Kenyon, for whom Harrison was then working at Gredington (see page 92), and subscriptions soon began to be collected from the gentry of Flintshire and Denbighshire.[1] On 25 October 1810 – even before a design was proposed – the foundation stone was laid amid much ceremony by Lord Kenyon.

Harrison had just been chosen as the architect. He first thought of a tall, battlemented tower, with some resemblance to the turrets of Caernarfon Castle, but he soon changed this to an Egyptian obelisk – which is thought to have been the first Egyptian-style monument in Britain. Harrison had, of course, seen Egyptian obelisks in Rome, but the Egyptian

[Figure 55]
The Jubilee Tower
on Moel Fammau,
1850.

style had only recently become fashionable in Britain – thanks in part to
the work of Napoleon's archaeologists, but also largely to Nelson's victory
at Aboukir Bay and the triumph of Sir Ralph Abercromby's army at
Alexandria. It also had overtones of eternal life, and was coming to be
regarded as the precursor of Greek architecture and, therefore, a pure source
of Classical inspiration.

The plan for an obelisk, standing on a broad base, some 50 feet square,
was approved in February 1811, but work did not begin until 1813. Suitable
stone had to be found, and the farm around Moel Fammau – which
belonged to the Crown – had then to be bought by Lord Kenyon, so that
it could be quarried. Harrison planned that the obelisk should be 115 feet
high, but the contractor, Thomas Penson of Wrexham, who was the father
of one of Harrison's former pupils, refused to build it, as drawn, without

[Figure 56]
One of Harrison's fourteen 'Testimonial' drawings, *c*.1815. Reproduced by courtesy of Cheshire Museums Service.

some form of insurance against losses. This support was not forthcoming, perhaps because a bridge, which Penson was building over the Dee at Overton, had just collapsed. The obelisk was therefore built in two diminishing stages, and turned out lower than intended. [Figure 55] Old prints suggest that in its setting, it looked quite impressive, but it is not certain that enough money was ever raised to finish it completely. A corner had to be rebuilt in 1846, and in October 1862 the obelisk collapsed. Its ruins were consolidated in 1970 and made into a viewing platform.

The end of the war against Napoleon was, however, the major stimulus to the designers of monuments in the early 1800s, and Harrison produced his fair share. The Cheshire Museums Service has 14 different designs for a 'Testimonial' to celebrate the defeat of Napoleon. Some are simple, but others show him indulging in Romantic daydreams – playing with geometric shapes and large-scale classical motifs, to produce designs, which might strike us as megalomaniac but which then would have been labelled 'sublime'. One has a Pantheon-type dome on a square base, surrounded by four Doric porticos; another leaves Rome altogether – for Egypt [Figure 56] and has a monumental pyramid with, on each side, a portico whose columns have lotus-flower capitals, and an obelisk at each corner.

In the twentieth century we came to think of war memorials as commemorations of the courage and skill of all – other ranks and officers – who had fought and died in the major conflicts from the Boer War onwards; however, in the eighteenth century and in the nineteenth century before the Crimean War it was only commanders who were publicly remembered by name. Harrison's first involvement in the design and construction of what one might call 'war-leader memorials' was only indirect.

He did not, as is often stated, *design* **Lord Hill's Column,** in **Shrewsbury**, to commemorate Shropshire's most famous living son.[*] The column is often attributed to him, but Colvin [2] makes clear that the idea for a fluted Doric column came from Edward Haycock – the 24-year-old architect son of the Shrewsbury builder, Hiram Haycock, who had come third in the competition for Chester County Gaol.

Lord Hills Column, Shrewsbury.

Hill had made a successful career in the Army, winning the respect of his superiors and the affection of his men and hence the nickname Daddy Hill. He had played a major role in the victories in the Peninsula War, and his return to Shrewsbury had been like a Roman triumph. After Napoleon's first abdication in 1814, he had been made Baron Hill of Hawkstone, but work had hardly begun on the monument, before he was recalled to the Continent, after Napoleon's escape from Elba, to become Wellington's second-in-command at Waterloo.

Edward Haycock had come second in the competition – the winner had been the sculptor Richard Westmacott – but won the commission to build the monument, on condition that Harrison should make some alterations to his column and be responsible for its construction. Harrison's alterations, however, were not minor: they involved the change from Roman Doric to the more fashionable Greek Doric, and the introduction of a high square

[Figure 57] Shrewsbury: Lord Hill's Column, *c.*1900. Reproduced by permission of Shropshire Archives.

[*] There was nothing new in the idea of a commemorative column. Trajan's Column in Rome had greatly impressed Harrison in the 1770s, and was to be replicated more or less in the Place Vendôme in Paris in 1810 to commemorate Napoleon's victories. The oldest column in England to celebrate a soldier is perhaps the Roman Doric Column of Victory, raised in 1727 in the park of Blenheim Palace to commemorate Marlborough's victory in December 1704.

pedestal with lions on large diagonally placed projections at the angles, to make the base look more stable. [Figure 57] The enormous first stone was laid in December 1814.

The monument is sturdily magnificent, a fluted Doric column 15 feet in diameter and 91 feet high. Its pedestal is decorated with a Latin inscription and a longer English one, celebrating Lord Hill's military skill and 'paternal care' for his soldiers. It carries on its top a 17-feet-high Coade stone statue of him in uniform. The 163 large sandstone blocks, each some 18 inches in depth, which form the shaft, were laid without mortar but fixed together with brass clamps.[3] The last stone was laid on 18 June 1816, symbolically the first anniversary of the battle of Waterloo, and the work was fully complete by September 1817. It cost £5,974.

The similar **Marquess of Anglesey's Column**, built at **Llanfairpwll** on the island of Anglesey on a hill overlooking the Menai Straits, was the work of Harrison alone; he was presumably commissioned because of his work in Shrewsbury. He designed it for the people of Anglesey and Caernarfon to commemorate, as the inscription reads, 'the distinguished military achievements of their countryman, Henry William, Marquess of Anglesey'.[4] The Marquess' family, the Pagets, were prominent gentry in Staffordshire, and had inherited estates in Anglesey, including the rich copper mines near Amlwch, in 1782, along with the house, Plas Newydd. Paget had played a prominent part as a cavalry commander in the Peninsular War and, when Napoleon escaped from Elba, he was appointed commander of the Allied cavalry in the Netherlands and at the battle of Waterloo.

The first of the Column's huge stones of 'Mona marble', a limestone from a quarry near Moelfre on Anglesey, was laid in June 1816, and it was completed, without mortar, in September 1817 at a cost of nearly £2,000. The stop-fluted Doric column, standing 91 feet high on a low square base, is visible both from the main road and from Plas Newydd. Originally it was crowned by no more than a square platform, which allows a splendid view of Snowdonia, but in 1860 a 12-feet-high bronze statue was added, showing the Marquess in uniform.

There was something of a mania for columns after the end of the Napoleonic Wars, but it appears from a letter, which he wrote in April 1819,[5] that Harrison had suggested, while in London in July 1818, that money would be better spent in building a purpose-designed home for the growing collections of the British Museum in London, which a couple of years before had acquired the Elgin Marbles. He had also given the Chancellor of the Exchequer sketches of a design for such a museum on the site of the Royal Mews – now occupied by the National Gallery on Trafalgar Square. However, the new museum building, with its impressive Ionic colonnades, was not begun until 1823, and then in Bloomsbury and to the designs of Robert Smirke.

A few years later Harrison designed a second monument on Anglesey –

[Figure 58]
Holyhead:
Commemorative
Gateway, 1850.

not a war memorial, but a **gateway at Holyhead** to commemorate the landing there of George IV on 7 August 1821. [Figure 58] The King was on his way to visit Ireland, but decided at short notice to visit Wales as well.[6] He stepped ashore on John Rennie's recently built Admiralty Pier, was met by the gentry of Anglesey and Caernarfon and stayed the night at Plas Newydd. The following day, however, the wind would not allow the royal yacht to sail on to Ireland, and it had to shelter behind Rennie's pier for five days, until a P&O steam packet could take the King to Dublin. Even before he left, a subscription had been launched for a memorial to this unplanned and unexpectedly long Royal Visit, and the first stone – of Mona marble – had been laid. Harrison was asked to produce a design, and the gateway to the pier was opened in August 1824. It had cost nearly £600. It is now inaccessible on the operational land of the ferry terminal, but can be seen at some distance from Victoria Road.

Harrison told Charles Cockerell in 1823 that he had considered an Egyptian design, but instead he designed a sort of Greek triumphal arch – rather like the Northgate in Chester. Each face has a pair of unfluted Doric columns, set between pilasters and carrying a full entablature with a bold cornice; this is topped by three stepped courses of masonry, forming a roof. Above the carriageway the triglyph frieze is replaced by a panel bearing a commemorative inscription in Welsh on one side and in Latin on the other. Like the Propylaea Gateway at Chester, it may appear to us, who live in a world of skyscrapers, to be rather small, but if we can measure it against human beings – and there is no better measure – it is impressive in its scale.

CHAPTER TWELVE

Last Houses, 1820–25

After a lull in 1817–18, about which no information, which might explain it, is available, Harrison's workload increased again in 1819, and he was thereafter busy for most of the rest of his life. His least significant work was the cast-iron veranda and conservatory, which he designed around 1820 at *Hoole House,* near Chester, for Lady Elizabeth Broughton, who was an enthusiastic gardener. The house was demolished in 1972, but is illustrated in the *Hoole Millennium Book* of 2000.

His first house after Grove House at Allerton was **Watergate House,** on **Watergate Street** in **Chester**, which he designed in 1820 for Henry Potts, for whom he had probably designed Glan-yr-Afon. The specification (and contract), dated 26 July 1820, mentions Harrison several times and is signed by Henry Potts and the builder William Cole.[1] The work cost about £4,000, and it is clear from the document that Cole was required to re-use many of the old materials from the previous house on the site.

By this time Potts was the Clerk of the Peace for the County. His father had died in 1817, so this house was probably his way – he was by then in his early forties – of marking his presence as one of Chester's leading citizens. It is one of the biggest private houses in the town and the finest of Harrison's three houses there. Standing originally in a large sloping garden (with good views westwards to the Clwydian Hills) just inside the Watergate, it occupies a corner site – which gives scope for an impressive entrance. It is built of good bricks and fits in well with most of the other houses on Watergate Street. It has recently been carefully restored for use as offices and is not open to the public. [Figure 59]

The house has three bays on both facades on either side of the corner, and two storeys of almost equal height above the stuccoed basement. A prominent cornice hides the hipped roofs. All the windows on both floors have 12-pane sashes – a welcome change, which can be seen in all Harrison's subsequent houses. The corner is cut back to create a wide convex quadrant, which contains the single-bay entrance in the form of a recessed Ionic porch; the first-floor window in a moulded architrave above gives some needed vertical emphasis. The cornice of the entablature of the porch is continued as a stucco band between the storeys all around the house. The service rooms were in the further end of the left-hand façade and in the basement.

The garden front has three widely spaced bays with a fashionable

segmental bow in the middle; all the ground-floor windows and the central one on the first floor are tripartite in form; they have 15-pane sashes between the simple square mullions – which, according to the specification, are of cast iron.

The front porch is part of a circular entrance lobby, which leads into one of the canted corners of the square hall; this is a simple but impressive atrium-like space which rises through both storeys of the house to an octagonal dome, topped with a tall lantern. [Figure 60] Almost opposite the front door are two columns between pilasters, which form a screen and carry a deep entablature, which divides the two storeys. They are made of wood, doubtless around a cast-iron core, and are painted to look like black marble. The diagonal axis of the entrance continues, in that to get to the reception rooms at the back of the house, one must turn half-right, go between the columns and then turn left or half-right. The left-hand room must have been the dining room, since it has only one entrance and the frieze of its cornice contains bunches of grapes. The cornices of the other two rooms – the drawing room (with the bow window) and the library, to which it is linked by double doors – are richly decorated with fashionable motifs, like the honeysuckle and the Greek key.

The plan of Watergate House suggests that Harrison, having set himself the challenge of designing a house, which was to be entered at one corner, rose to meet it with some panache to create a memorable sequence of spaces.

[Figure 59]
Chester: Watergate
House – Exterior,
2004.

[Figure 60]
Chester: Watergate House – The Hall, 2004.
Reproduced by courtesy of the owner.

He was clearly pleased with the outcome, because he told Cockerell in 1823 that the design had been copied in 1821 for a house on Piccadilly in London.

Harrison's last commission on a country estate in Cheshire came in 1821, when he was asked to design **Tilstone Lodge** for Admiral John Halliday. [Figure 61] The Admiral had just inherited the large Tilstone estate, through his mother, and in consequence took her family name of Tollemache. However, though he was a wealthy man, with an estate in Antigua as well as another in Suffolk, he did not want a seat in Cheshire – merely a house, as he said in a letter of 1822, as 'an occasional Residence to receive my tenants and for shooting and hunting'.[2] The house was built on a new site and stands in an attractive, landscaped park. It is still a private house and not open to the public.

It looks like an attractively simple suburban villa, but has a large service wing and stables, half-hidden to the left. It is built of brick, stuccoed and scored to look like ashlar in 12-inch courses, and has two storeys of almost equal height. The only Classical details are the four unfluted Doric columns of the porte cochère on the entrance front. This façade has three widely spaced bays; a narrower fourth bay to the right is slightly set back and, on its return wall, projects in the still fashionable bow – with French windows, which light the drawing room and give a good view of the park. In front of it is a delicate cast-iron veranda, which supports a balcony on the first floor. All the windows on both floors have plain jambs and 12-pane sashes, while the French windows, as at Broomhall, have bronze glazing bars, which allow larger panes of glass.

The interior was somewhat altered, probably between the Wars: the wall between the entrance hall and the top-lit stairhall was removed, so that they now form one large room with a new staircase. All the main rooms on the

ground floor are pleasantly spacious, and two have bows, and most have doors and shutters with planted mouldings and their original plaster cornices with Greek motifs – the one in the dining room, though, has bunches of grapes.

[Figure 61]
Tilstone Lodge:
Entrance Front,
2004.

Harrison was also prepared to design houses in the Gothick idiom at this time – there was no 'battle of the styles' before Pugin in the 1840s – and, probably while he was designing Tilstone Lodge, made some alterations in the east wing of **Chirk Castle**. This had been badly damaged during the Civil War and was rebuilt in the 1670s, with an impressive gallery on the first floor above a deep loggia. In the 1770s the house was brought up to date with a fine suite of Classical reception rooms, designed by Joseph Turner. Fashion changed again, and in 1796 a visitor regretted that much had been lost of the 'Character of an antient Baron's Castle'.[3] Some 20 years later, Mrs Charlotte Myddelton Biddulph commissioned Harrison, during the minority of her son, to rectify this fault by converting the loggia and one of the towers into a suite of Gothick rooms for the family. It is in part of the National Trust house, but is not open to the public.

Harrison built a single-storey corridor in front of the loggia; he ceiled this and the other rooms with simple lath and plaster vaults, but in the Drawing Room in the tower he went interestingly further. [Figure 62] The room is

[Figure 62]
Chirk Castle:
ceiling of the
Drawing Room in
the private wing,
2004. Reproduced
by courtesy of the
owner.

D-shaped, so he re-used motifs, reminiscent of the Shire Hall of Lancaster Castle – a semi-circular vaulted ceiling and a wide panelled arch over the fireplace recess, which recalls the great arch over the judges' bench.

Mrs Myddelton's son in due course followed the next fashion to prefer something more 'correct' and in the 1840s commissioned Pugin to gothicise the whole house. Pugin condemned Harrison's work, because it did not look genuinely medieval. He was right, of course, but sham authenticity was not the priority of Harrison or of his client; they were content with the associations of arches and vaults.

Harrison's last significant work on a gentleman's country house anywhere was at *Hardwick Grange*, in Shropshire. The house belonged to General Lord Hill, and it was he who commissioned Harrison late in 1821 to alter the front of the house and add a dining room. He asked for a Gothick design, probably because he appreciated that this style was becoming fashionable and liked the overtones of long-standing gentry status which were associated with it. The work cost £4,911. The house was further extended towards the end of the nineteenth century, but demolished in 1931,[4] and all that remains of Harrison's work is a battlemented gateway lodge on the west side of the A49.

A photograph in the Shropshire Archives at Shrewsbury[5] shows what must be Harrison's work at the big house – a two-storey, five-bay wing, where all the major windows had a single mullion and transom under a square hoodmould. Between the projecting end-bays a single storey, battlemented loggia projected further and provided a balcony for the first-floor rooms. It calls to mind Harrison's rather two-dimensional façade for the Debtors' Wing at Lancaster Castle.

It is also similar to some of the designs which he was making at about that time for the President and Fellows of **Magdalen College, Oxford**, in response to what he thought was another Gothick commission.[6] To the north of the College's medieval Cloisters stands the so-called **New Building,** which had been built in 1733 in a restrained Palladian manner with two storeys above an arcade. It had always been intended to connect it with the Cloisters and thus to form a new Great Quadrangle, and so its ends were left unfinished and untidy. Designs were sought from several eminent architects, but nothing was done for nearly a century – largely because the Fellows could never agree whether the linking blocks should match the Gothic cloister or the Georgian wing.

In 1820 they decided to seek Harrison's advice – which suggests the respect in which he was held – and he replied that the work should be Gothick in its style. He also understood that he had been asked to provide drawings for the alteration of the medieval buildings and the creation of the quadrangle. Having visited the College some

[Figure 63]
Oxford: Magdalen
College –
Harrison's
completion of the
New Building,
2004.

years before and relying on memory and a few drawings sent to him by the College's President, he began in 1822 to produce some elevations for a Library and Fellows' Building on the Great Quadrangle – mostly in the manner of the debtors' wing at Lancaster Castle. No-one, however, mentioned to him that the London architect, Joseph Parkinson,[7] had also been consulted and had in fact been appointed the College's architect in 1821. Parkinson proceeded to demolish the north walk of the medieval Cloisters, and this provoked violent protests, reported several times in the *Gentleman's Magazine* during 1822. When Harrison read about these, he protested to the College, but agreed to send his drawings, which also included some for the completion of the ends of the New Building in a straightforward Classical manner. These drawings are now in the College's collection.[8]

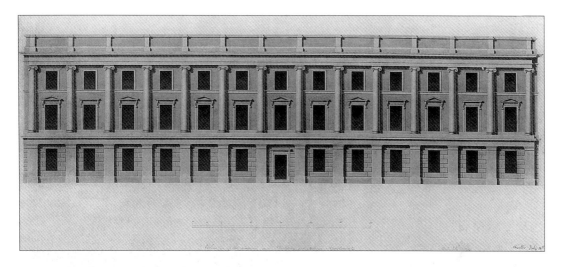

[Figure 64] Oxford: Magdalen College – Harrison's drawing of a proposed Classical block for the (unbuilt) Great Quadrangle, 1822. Reproduced by permission of The President and Fellows of Magdalen College, Oxford.

The Fellows accepted his drawings for the New Building, and his design was built in 1824, at the rather high cost of almost £2,600. [Figure 63] The last three bays at each end now project slightly, and the arcades are replaced there by square-headed recessed panels. The original cornice and attic are continued, and the new windows match the proportions of those of the older building, though their details are simpler. It is a gentlemanly solution, for which Parkinson took the credit.[9] (He must also take the blame for specifying a stone, which has weathered to a very different colour from that of the earlier work.)

Nothing, however, came of the proposal to link the Cloister to the New Building with a new quadrangle, and this is perhaps the greatest 'might-have-been' of Harrison's career. In addition to his executed plans for the ends of the New Building he also produced a Classical design for one wing of the new quadrangle, which is an improved re-working of Broomhall. [Figure 64] It has 13 bays and two-and-a-half storeys. The rusticated basement has Tuscan pilasters, which support giant Ionic columns in front of the ashlar upper storeys. The cornices and plain balustrade give the façade a marked horizontal emphasis, but this is well balanced by the pilasters and columns to create a fine, well-proportioned design of restrained grandeur – perhaps, even, Harrison's best Classical façade. Harrison was not, to my mind, a 'reluctant Goth', as has been suggested;[10] he was clearly prepared to design in the Gothick idiom, but does seem to have felt more at home when using the Classical language.

His last work for a private client, the so-called **Citadel** near **Hawkstone** – designed in 1824 for Sir Rowland Hill, the great nephew of General Lord Hill – is another work in the Gothick manner. [Figure 65] It is not part of the famous landscaped park at Hawkstone, but was built as a dower house for Sir Rowland's mother. It is now a small country house hotel.

It is a nine-bay building of two roughly equal storeys, faced with large

[Figure 65]
Hawkstone:
The Citadel, 2004.

blocks of a red sandstone, quarried locally. The centre is dominated by a tall, round tower, from which the entrance porch projects slightly; on either side, short wings splay back to a slightly lower tower at each end, so that the building has a V-shaped plan. (The three towers are a punning reference to the Hills' coat of arms.) The porch has a four-centred arch, and this is echoed by the window above it and by the first-floor windows in the other towers; all the other windows have a mullion and transom under a square hoodmould. Cross-shaped arrow-loops and battlements give the building a slightly military air, which is complemented by the battlemented terrace in front. The Citadel stands in a dominating position, and is so placed both to enjoy the wide view to the north-east and also to be seen, as a picturesque feature, within the landscape. It composes well from various viewpoints – not just like a façade cut out of cardboard, as at Hardwick Grange, but as a solid mass of carefully contrasted shapes.

The porch leads through a hexagonal, plaster-vaulted entrance hall to one corner of the fine rectangular stairhall – the centre of the house – where the stone staircase is cantilevered from two walls around an open, top-lit well. The reception rooms, in both wings, have fireplaces with four-centred arches, and their ceilings too are attractive: the one in the dining room has bunches of grapes on the main beams, while the one in the drawing room, although it is flat, is decorated with what look like vaulting ribs.

[Figure 66]
Chester: St
Martin's Lodge,
2005.

Harrison also designed a house for himself – **St Martin's Lodge** in **Nicholas Street, Chester;** the land had been granted to him by the County 'in gratitude for his professional services'. The house was probably begun in 1822, and was certainly finished by 9 November 1823, when Charles Cockerell spent an evening there. In 1857 Harrison's daughter, Anne, bequeathed the house to be the rectory for the recently combined parishes of St Bridget and St Martin. It is now used as offices and is not open to the public.

It is a simple villa, built of brick but rendered and scored to give 15-inch 'courses' on the three principal sides. [Figure 66] It has two storeys of more or less equal height, separated by a simple cornice, three widely spaced windows on each main façade, and shallow hipped roofs with overhanging eaves. All the windows have plain jambs, and almost all still have 12-pane sashes. The garden façade to the south, from which Harrison will have had a good view of his buildings at the Castle, has a slightly projecting centre with its own roof and eaves, which form an open pediment and give a central vertical emphasis, which was just becoming fashionable. This emphasis is further strengthened by the projection of a shallow canted bay, which has full-height sash windows and provides a balcony for a bedroom on the first floor. (The square bay to the left probably dates from after 1857.) The kitchen and service rooms were on the north, above a basement, and faced onto a small service yard, approached from Blackfriars.

Inside the house much of the original interior decoration remains. The square entrance lobby leads to the top-lit hall-cum-stairhall, where the simple staircase, with two stick balusters per tread, rises up the right-hand wall under a segmental ceiling. The reception rooms are on the left, overlooking the garden, and the dining room in the far corner has a segment-headed recess for the sideboard, and a fireplace, similar in style to the reeded doorcases. Charles Cockerell, who saw the house when he visited Harrison, wrote in his diary that it was 'well conceived, broad, elegant and simple'.[11] This is conventional praise – the house is austerely pleasant rather than outstanding – and Cockerell went on to confide his view that Harrison was better at the exteriors than the interiors of buildings.

This must be true: with the exception of the Shire Halls, the Lyceum and the Portico Library and perhaps the hall of Watergate House, Harrison designed no memorable rooms, let alone coherent suites of varied internal spaces – but, working mostly for a middle-class, rather than an aristocratic, clientèle, he was probably never asked to do so. However, his houses are always well sited to enjoy a good view, and his plans will have worked well; although the interior decoration of most of the rooms in his houses is limited to a skirting board, a dado rail and a simple cornice, to doors with planted mouldings set in reeded architraves, to panelled window shutters, and simple, well positioned fireplaces, they are always well proportioned, and drawing rooms often have bow windows. They merely need to be complemented by decent furniture and generous curtains.

The Citadel near Hawkstone was Harrison's last design for a building, as distinct from one for a bridge. The challenge of producing a small house-cum-eye-catcher led him to propose an attractive simplification of his rather rambling Gothick plans for Lowther Hall (see Appendix B). St Martin's Lodge is interesting, and Watergate House is second to none of his villas. The Drawing Room at Chirk Castle is a clever re-working of the Shire Hall at Lancaster – but his *Gothick* designs for the Magdalen College quadrangle and for Hardwick Grange are little more than a re-hash of his Debtors' Wing at Lancaster Castle. It is difficult not to conclude that some of his last designs are merely repetitions of earlier plans by an old man, but I think that Summerson was too harsh to say that 'many of his later buildings are very tame.' His *Classical* design for the new quadrangle at Magdalen College was second to few in its day. Nevertheless, Harrison was probably aware of some slowing down. He must have known that he had been passed over in 1817, in favour of George Moneypenny, for the work of designing the Sessions House at Knutsford (a striking building, which used to be thought to be Harrison's work) and that Moneypenny had been asked to reinstate the east wing of Tabley House after a fire in 1819. When he was invited in 1824 to submit plans for the proposed Royal Institution at Manchester (now the City Art Gallery), he declined on the grounds of increasing old age.

CHAPTER THIRTEEN

Cheshire Bridges, 1800–1826

There is a pleasing – almost Classical – symmetry to what is known of Harrison's professional career: his first work was Skerton Bridge in Lancaster, and his last designs were for two bridges in Chester, one old and one new; one which he saw through to completion, and one which he designed, but which others realised after his death. Both of them were commissions in the public sector, which brought him some trouble, as extraneous political rivalries and private interests intruded into technical matters and public concerns.

These bridges were designed by him in his capacity as County Surveyor, a post he only held formally after 1815, but the order books of the Cheshire JPs show that he had been involved in work on several other bridges before then. In some cases he did no more than inspect work, done by others, but in February 1800 he was asked to prepare plans and specifications for five bridges in the Bucklow and Macclesfield Hundreds.[1] Of these **Hug Bridge**, which now carries the A523 over the River Dane, involved no more than the widening of an earlier bridge, while **Allostock Bridge**, which carries the A50 over the Crow Brook, has rusticated voussoirs, but is dated 1821. From this I infer that Harrison decided that a mid-eighteenth-century bridge did not need significant work, but that repairs were considered necessary 20 years later.

The other three bridges, **Lindford Bridge** and **Radnor Bridge** over the River Dane and **Oversley Ford Bridge** over the Bollin, now carry minor roads and are very similar. They are about 24 feet wide and built of well dressed sandstone; they each have a segmental arch with a span of about 50 feet and a rise of about 10 feet, with voussoirs which interlock with the stones in the spandrels. Their structural design, their good proportions and austere manner persuade me that they were certainly designed by Harrison.

For several years he appears to have done no more bridge work, but then in 1809 there were complaints from the Lancashire JPs to their Cheshire counterparts that the medieval bridge over the Mersey at *Warrington* was so low that it was causing flooding in some parts of the town. A committee of three JPs from each County was therefore set up, and in July 1810 they consulted Harrison. After some delays, which annoyed them and led them to wonder whether Telford's plan for a cast-iron bridge might be appropriate,[2] he met them in January 1811, and in November 1812 William

Cole contracted to build a new *Mersey Bridge* with a single shallow span of 140 feet, rising some 6 feet above the top of the abutments – all for the low price of £3,000. The first stone of the abutments was laid in June 1813, and the bridge was opened in 1817.

The reason for the low price was that the arch of the bridge was of timber, not of stone. We do not know why. The townspeople petitioned for a stone bridge, but the JPs refused. Did they – in war-time – want a low cost above all else, or did Harrison – the son of a joiner – want to try out a new idea? Whatever the answer, the bridge was of novel design.[3] It was composed of two parallel arches of red American pine, five feet thick at the crown and seven at the abutments, set 19 feet apart and cross-braced together. Each arch was laminated, that is, made of five super-imposed curving ribs, each constructed of thick planks, joined lengthwise and made to curve by cast-iron wedges, forced into deep slots cut into the top surface. Each plank was fastened to its neighbours, above and below, by thick bolts. On these arches further timbers, of oak, were fixed to carry the road and footways.

There are in Warrington Library two (possibly inaccurate) sketches of the bridge, made around 1820 by a local artist, Robert Booth.[4] They show that it looked quite graceful, but also – there is no other word – flimsy. In practical terms, it lacked the necessary stiffness, both across its width and especially lengthwise: the ratio of at least 1:10 between its rise and its span was daring to the point of recklessness – a ratio of about 1:5 was normal – and before long it caused problems. The Lancashire historian, Edward Baines[5] stated as early as 1825 that 'as a timber bridge, this structure does credit to the architect, Mr Harrison of Chester, but indications are already visible of the insufficiency of the material, and the impolicy of the counsels which could, at this time of day, prefer timber to stone, will soon be made manifest by the necessity for a new one'. He was not wrong; one abutment soon started to crack, and a pier had to built in the river to carry a pair of trusses to support the arch, which was beginning to sag. Finally the bridge was demolished in 1837 and replaced by a stone bridge of three arches, costing £5,500.

However, in 1815, while the Cheshire magistrates were still pleased by the cheapness of the Warrington Bridge, they asked Harrison to design a similar but smaller one to replace the medieval *Cranage Bridge*, where the turnpike from Warrington to Kidsgrove (now the A50) crossed the River Dane. J. H. Hanshall, in 1817, mentions the old stone bridge and 'a wooden one erected in its stead, after plans by Mr Harrison, the County architect',[6] but the bridge must have shared the same fate as the one at Warrington, because the present bridge has a semi-elliptical arch of red sandstone and probably dates from the mid-nineteenth century.

These two bridges must be reckoned not only as significant innovations – I know of no earlier examples – but also as significant failures in Harrison's career. Laminated timber arches were used at King's Cross station in

London in 1851, but they were covered by a roof and were roughly semi-circular in form; even so they were replaced in steel in 1869. However, these two bridges were Harrison's only failures, and he was more successful in the last two, which he designed at Chester.

The seven-arched **Dee Bridge** at **Chester** (which can be seen in Figure 18) was, like all medieval bridges then, becoming inadequate to carry growing volumes of traffic. The problem had become more urgent after the Act of Union in 1800 united Ireland with Great Britain, since the Post Office was anxious to speed the mails to and from Dublin. Thomas Telford's consequent improvements of the Holyhead Road west of Shrewsbury threatened to attract north of England traffic (and therefore prosperity) away from Chester. A competition for a new bridge was therefore held in 1808 and was won by the Wrexham architect, Thomas Penson. Nothing, however, was done for ten years.

Then, in September 1818, the County's Grand Jury passed a resolution in favour of a new bridge close to the old site. Penson's career had meanwhile collapsed with his Overton bridge in 1813, so they asked Harrison for a design and cost-estimates. He proposed an iron bridge, but the County's Bridge Committee wanted a stone one. The problem was exacerbated, since the site of any new County bridge close to the old one would have been within the City's jurisdiction, and so in the end Harrison proposed no more than a seven-foot widening of the old bridge, mostly on the upstream side. He produced many detailed plans, now in the Cheshire County Record Office,[7] but nothing was done until 1825, when plain new arches were built in front of the first three arches (from the city bank) on the upstream side and in front of the seventh arch on the downstream side; a footway with an iron balustrade was then corbelled-out on the upstream side.

In the meantime the Cheshire magistrates had sent a Bill to Parliament in 1819, asking for authority to improve the main road from Chester to Holyhead, with a bridge[*] at Conwy to replace the dangerous ferry. At the back of their minds was the idea of a totally new bridge at Chester downstream of the Castle and outside the City boundary. There was, of course, opposition in the town to the idea of a new bridge, since it would lead to a reduction in the value of properties at the lower end of Bridge Street. Furthermore, the creation of a new road to link it to the centre – the first major change to the Roman and medieval street-system in Chester – would involve the demolition of properties, including the church of St Bridget. Nevertheless, the JPs plucked up their courage, and in 1824 applied for an Act of Parliament to build a new bridge, the **Grosvenor Bridge** in **Chester**.[8] It was passed in June 1825.

---

[*] This is the graceful suspension bridge, designed by Thomas Telford and opened in 1826, which still stands in front of Conwy Castle.

At the same time they also asked Harrison to draw up plans for the creation of what is now Grosvenor Street. He also produced designs – both Gothick and Grecian – for a new St Bridget's church opposite the Gateway to the Castle, but the church was built to a simple Grecian design by William Cole – rather like Harrison's chapel at High Legh. Grosvenor Street was laid out from January 1827, but nothing from Harrison's time survives there.[*]

Harrison had been asked in 1824 to produce designs for a bridge, with a height above low water of 60 feet – to allow the passage of ships carrying corn to the mills by the old bridge – on a site where the river was 200 feet wide. He considered an iron bridge, with a segmental arch of 170 feet, flanked by stone arches. This had an estimated cost of £26,000, but both he and the County's Bridge Committee preferred the idea of a stone bridge. In the Cheshire Record Office[9] there is a drawing of November 1824, perhaps in George Latham's hand, which shows a bridge with a single stone arch, spanning 200 feet and rising 27 feet from the abutments. This gives a ratio between the rise and the span of about 1:7, which was daring to the point of foolhardiness, but Harrison also produced plans for two more stone bridges: one had three tall arches with a 70-foot span, at an estimated cost of some £15,000, while the other had a single segmental arch, spanning 200 feet with a rise of 40 feet and costing some £23,000.

Needless to say, the Committee had reservations about such a large single-span bridge. Harrison, nevertheless, pursued the idea of a single arch – which he knew would have the longest span in the world – and approached the engineer, James Trubshaw, the latest in a long dynasty of masons and surveyors in Staffordshire, and a man with a reputation for competence, 'integrity and business-like habits'[10]. Trubshaw visited Chester in February and April 1825 and supported Harrison's basic idea and his estimate of costs. So too did John Rennie, the son of Harrison's friend, the great engineer, whom he had first met at Skerton in 1784.

Harrison was also thinking about materials; he had been impressed by the strength of the Mona marble limestone, used for the Marquess of Anglesey's Column and the Memorial at Holyhead, and the contractor for the latter brought him samples. From these Trubshaw had an accurate scale model made of Harrison's arch, which he brought to Chester, and displayed in the hope of proving that the real thing would stand without collapsing. (The model was restored by the Chester Civic Trust in 1979 and now stands against the grass bank above Castle Drive.)

The Committee still had doubts, first about costs, but also about the engineering aspects of the design, since boreholes on the site had shown that there was no rock before a depth of 38 feet. Despite this the Committee

---

[*] However, the Grosvenor Museum in that street contains a small Harrison archive, with some of his drawings and a good portrait of him, in oil by Henry Wyatt and dated 1820.

was prepared to entertain the idea of a 200-foot arch, built of brick, faced with stone and filled with rubble, proposed by the engineer, Marc Brunel, at a cost of £35,520. His son, the later more famous Isambard Kingdom Brunel, apparently even claimed that a bridge could be built of rubble-stone for £10,000. The Committee was sceptical, and Brunel's assurances were not very convincing.

All this vacillation, though, was too much for Harrison, and in January 1826 he wrote to the Committee, resigning from the job, on the grounds of 'my advanced age' – he was 81 – 'and the infirmities attending it'. He continued: ' I trust the Committee will have no difficulty … in procuring a younger and more competent person for the purpose, who may be able to attend to the progress of this arduous work and live to see it completed … I shall view with pleasure the successful progress of a work which has so long occupied my thoughts and had my earnest wishes.' He handed over his drawings to his former pupil, William Cole, but the latter played little part in the building of the bridge. Once the principle of a single stone arch had been accepted, the details of its construction were worked out by engineers. Harrison's final bill was paid in January 1827, and he was thereafter kept regularly informed of progress.

In May 1826 Telford visited Chester at the request of the Committee and suggested another site about 100 yards downstream, where new soundings had shown that the underlying rock was close to the surface. His estimate of costs for Harrison's bridge was £50,698. In August 1826 the Committee voted by 13 to 6 in favour of Harrison's plan and Telford's costings. The construction work was entrusted to Trubshaw with Jesse Hartley as the clerk of works. He was the son of the West Riding's Bridgemaster and was already Surveyor to the Liverpool Dock Trustees, but his contract allowed him to work outside that town. Hartley accepted to manage the project, on the basis of following Harrison's design for the appearance of the bridge, but with liberty to make changes to the internal construction. In the event, he lowered the abutments by one foot and raised the crown of the arch by one foot – thereby making the rise of the arch correspond to the 42 feet, which the elder John Rennie had advocated for a span of 200 feet. Otherwise he followed Harrison's monumental design faithfully, but it is arguable that it was he who ensured its structural success.

The Earl Grosvenor was pleased to lay the foundation stone and to accept that the bridge should be named after his family. The ceremony took place on 1 October 1827, in the presence of the new Bishop of Chester, Dr Charles Blomfield, and the great and good of the County. Harrison had asked to be excused on the grounds of 'his indisposition arising from his great age'. Work on the south abutment was begun in July 1828. Hartley – wisely, to my mind – chose to use Harrison's alternative and more massive design, rather than have a pair of somewhat skinny Doric columns to carry the entablature. The north abutment was completed late in 1829, and then

Trubshaw's impressive wooden centring for the arch, supported from four stone piers in the river, was built. The lowest voussoirs were laid with thick sheets of lead between them, and on 10 December 1830 the keystone was carefully placed, tapped down gently between strips of lead smeared with a lubricant putty, made of white lead and oil, until it was in the right position. This symbolic event was marked by a treat for the workmen, costing the generous sum of £21. The bridge was formally opened by Princess Victoria, the future Queen, in October 1832 and finally completed in the following year. When the centring was removed, the thrust of the arch compressed the malleable lead, and – remarkably – the crown of the arch settled a little over two inches – less than what Hartley had expected for an arch of that span and rise. He signed the certificate of completion on 23 November 1833. The work had cost just under £50,000.

We have become so used to seeing photographs of wide spans in striking landscapes, created by the use of reinforced concrete, that we have become somewhat blasé, but in 1833 this gateway to the city for river traffic, with its clear masonry span of 200 feet, must have been literally breathtaking. It is still impressive. [Figure 67] In Mordaunt Crook's beautifully apt phrase[11] – 'soaring like a rainbow' over the river Dee – the Grosvenor Bridge has both 'noble simplicity and quiet grandeur'. The segmental arch had the longest span of any stone arch in the world, and kept this distinction until 1864. The structure is 36 feet wide, and most of the stones, of which its

[Figure 67] Chester: Grosvenor Bridge, c.1835. Reproduced by courtesy of Cheshire Museums Service.

spandrels and abutments are constructed, are at least 18 inches deep, but the structure nevertheless appears light, because the arch itself is built of a pale limestone and is nearly six times longer than its width. Furthermore, the darker gritstone spandrels are set back twice behind the arch-ring, and only the cornice of the Doric entablature of the abutments passes over the crown of the arch, rising very slightly to the centre. This apparent lightness is further emphasised by the contrast with the massiveness of the projecting abutments, itself stressed by the round-headed niches, hollowed-out in their faces, and by the heavily rusticated retaining walls, which curve back on each side. This understated elegance is typical of the best of Harrison's work and a worthy memorial to his taste and skill.

* * *

Thomas Harrison never saw his bridge completed. He died at home, aged 84, on 29 March 1829, and was buried on 6 April in a vault in the churchyard of the new St Bridget's church. This was demolished in 1892, but its churchyard remained, only to be cleared in the summer of 1964, before Nicholas Street was widened. The family vault was then found, under a plain slab; inside were three coffins, two covered in lead and one – perhaps that of his son John who had died in 1802 – of simple wood. They were re-buried in the City Cemetery at Blacon. His daughters died, unmarried, in 1842 and 1857, so he has no descendants; nor did he found a dynasty of architects. If we are looking for his monument, we must look around at his work.

Conclusion: The Significance of Thomas Harrison

There are two portraits of Thomas Harrison on public display in Chester and a bust in Manchester, but the most widely available image of him is in the database of the National Portrait Gallery in London. [Figure 68] It is a lithograph, entitled 'To the Magistrates, Noblemen and Gentlemen of Cheshire this Portrait of Thomas Harrison, Esq., to whose Taste the County is indebted for its Principal Architectural Embellishments, is inscribed by their humble Servt, A R Burt, Miniature Painter, Chester, May 1 1824'.[1] The picture appears as a kindly caricature, but the flattering dedication shows the regard and esteem in which Harrison was held by most of his contemporaries in Chester. So too does the fact that, a fortnight after his burial, the churchwardens returned to his widow the £15 fee for a burial plot 'as a testimonial of the great estimation in which that gentleman's abilities were held by the Rector and parishioners of St Bridget.'[2]

There had already been an obituary in the *Chester Chronicle* of 3 April 1829, which spoke of 'this highly distinguished artist' who 'in his private life … was deservedly held in high estimation; and in his professional character had few equals'. Harrison's death was noted in the *Lancaster Gazette* of 11 April, and this was followed on 18 April by an obituary, based on the one published in Chester. There was as well an obituary for a national audience in the *Gentleman's Magazine* of May 1829, which too was copied almost word for word from the *Chester Chronicle*. A biographical sketch with a number of flattering references to his work appeared in Joseph Hemingway's 1831 *History of the City of Chester*.[3] In the 1850s Harrison was mentioned in the *Dictionary* of the Architectural Publication Society and even in Michaud's *Biographie universelle*, published in Paris, where his name appears between John Harrison, the inventor of the chronometer, and William Henry Harrison, the ninth President of the USA.

It is clear that Harrison was well regarded by some of the better-known architects of his day, whom he had met during his rare visits to London.[4] He was an acquaintance of the collector and connoisseur, Charles Towneley, and may have met him in Rome, since their stays overlapped in 1769–72. They certainly corresponded about the Elgin Marbles in 1803.

However, he was not an associate of the Royal Academy, nor a member of any of the London-based architectural societies. He does not appear to have tried to make a career in the capital; this has surprised most historians and will be discussed later.

We know that Charles Cockerell had long admired Harrison's work and, at the beginning of a brilliant career, after meeting him at his home in November 1823, went so far as to write in his diary, that Harrison had 'a spark divine'.[5] A few years later he added the note that Harrison was 'undoubtedly the noblest genius in architecture we have had'.[6] It is sad that by 1823 Harrison was nearly 80 – too late for praise to matter much, perhaps, though it would probably have been welcome. Cockerell may well have spoken to Harrison's face, as he wrote in his diary, of his 'noble mind, lofty and extensive views',[7] but it

To the Magistrates Noblemen and Gentlemen of Cheshire this Portrait of Thomas Harrison Esq.ʳ to whose Taste the County is indebted for its Principal Architectural Embellishments is inscribed by their humble Serv.ᵗ A.R. Burt. Miniature Painter Chester May 1ˢᵗ 1824.

[Figure 68] Thomas Harrison by A. R. Burt, 1824. Reproduced by permission of Cheshire and Chester Archives and Local Studies.

is doubtful that he would have added the further comment, which appears in his diary – namely, that these views were 'little improved by study'. The words are unconsciously condescending, such as one might expect from the confident, well-educated, much-travelled son of a successful and well-regarded architect: to him Harrison was a man of considerable natural talent, of noble genius even, but essentially a self-taught man, rather than conventionally educated – a fine craftsman, but not really a gentleman. It is in the light of such a comment as this that we have to see Harrison's apparent reluctance to leave Chester and try his luck in London.

* * *

Cockerell spoke of a 'spark divine'. What might he have meant: the quality of Harrison's mind or the quality of his architecture? Perhaps both. Colvin sums up Harrison's spark in these words: ' His bold sense of mass, his concern with the quality of masonry and his capacity to design in three dimensions set his work apart from the stereotyped Gothic boxes and

Grecian porticos characteristic of so much early-nineteenth-century British architecture'.[8] I can do little more than gloss and nuance that praise.

About 40 years ago, a famous scientist wrote of another famous scientist – the names do not matter – that 'his genius was to enrich the soil, not to bring new land into cultivation'. One can, however, say of Harrison that he had both sorts of genius. He certainly enriched the soil. As an architect working within the Classical conventions of his time, he was never less than competent. He followed the fashions and was able to recycle his ideas with some variations from building to building. Moreover, several of his works – Watergate House and Woodbank and his libraries in Liverpool and Manchester, for example – are elegantly simple; while some, like his two Shire Halls and those same two libraries, contain spaces of considerable interest.

Harrison also brought new land into cultivation – as a pioneer of what we call the Greek Revival. The assessments of modern architectural historians, like David Watkin and Giles Worsley, are unambiguous; the former praised him as the 'finest' of the architects who revived the forms of Greek architecture,[9] and the latter described him as 'the first English architect to grasp the full potential of the Greek Revival…[a man with a] thorough, but unpedantic, understanding of Greek architecture', adding that 'he created some of the finest neo-classical architecture of the Regency'.[10]

In many cases what the Georgians called 'Grecian' architecture was little more than a new source of fashionable decorative details for use within the 'antique manner' tradition, but to some people, including Harrison, it also had overtones of Periclean Athens. In the portico of the Chester Shire Hall, and above all in the Gateway to the Castle he sought to create sculptural works of monumental grandeur, which should be worthy of a place on the Acropolis. It has, though, to be asked how relevant such buildings, for all their Ionic elegance or Doric solemnity, were to Georgian England. Harrison was certainly among the very first to introduce Greek motifs, but he also seems to have been the first to realise their limitations in the real world of some 2,000 years later. He was never a pedant, striving at all costs after archaeological accuracy; he was never a fanatic, seeking to use Greek motifs in all circumstances.

Rather, he simplified Greek forms – often using unfluted columns – and within a few years he gave them up altogether, except for monumental public commissions. Colonnades and porticos look very fine on palaces and public buildings, but are of little practical value for private houses, which stand at 53° North rather than 38°, and whose weather comes from the Irish Sea rather than the Aegean. Furthermore, if one is to be true to the Greek tradition, one is limited to single-storey buildings without fine internal spaces or windows to the outside world. There is scope for cheating, thanks to giant columns and hidden mezzanines, but the Greek Revival, when taken to its logical conclusion as the sole source for contemporary design,

represented a narrowing of the classical repertoire; it became a stylistic cul-
de-sac, and 'noble simplicity and quiet grandeur' degenerated all too often
into boring monotony and frigid monumentality. Harrison knew that
architecture is more than designing façades; that it is primarily the art of
using structures to create spaces. He introduced Greek forms to Great
Britain, he explored them and employed them, and then after 1815 discarded
them except in a handful of cases. It was left to the next but one generation
– to men like Cockerell and Smirke – to develop them further in major
public commissions, but they could only do so by using them as the
Romans, but not the Greeks, had done – with arches, not lintels, and with
vaults (not to mention wrought-iron beams) to span large spaces.

* * *

Harrison was certainly more than just an architect, but was he 'primarily
of an engineering bent', as Summerson surmised? Perhaps, but probably
not. The unfortunate split between architects and engineers was only just
beginning in his middle years, though it was soon to be exacerbated by the
wish of many architects to be considered artists. His work shows clearly
that he was interested in galleried spaces within larger spaces, and in the
structures needed to cover wide rooms or create spacious domes. He was
interested in the structural aspects of buildings and sometimes, as in the
rusticated lintels of the Shire Hall or in the arch of the Northgate in Chester,
in showing how the buildings, which he had designed, were actually
constructed. He was certainly interested in using available new materials,
like bronze window frames, fire-proof ceilings and cast-iron balusters and
heating pipes. However, he does not appear to have done detailed designs
for structural ironwork, let alone thought much about the strengths and
weaknesses of wrought and cast iron.

Harrison was above all a 'man of stone', and Cockerell understood this
in his comments on the Northgate at Chester. He stood in awe of stone
and its massiveness – a view inspired, perhaps, as much by Pennine
Yorkshire as by Piranesi – and he sought to express this massiveness
whenever possible, in large blocks of stone and in monolithic columns, even
to the detriment of the proportions of some of his façades. Nothing,
however, suggests that he was deeply interested in analysing and
understanding structures *per se*, in the hope of moving, cautiously, beyond
current practice. The single stone arch of the Grosvenor Bridge was, I
believe, a consciously daring response to a half-perceived challenge, but the
dare-devil boldness of his timber bridges beggars belief and soon found its
nemesis.

* * *

The major question implicit in most comments on Harrison is why he never
moved to London, but stayed in Chester; it has exercised the mind of every

historian from Canon Blomfield to Sir John Summerson, but I am not sure that the question is appropriate. There is a danger of seeing Harrison with minds, developed not in the eighteenth century, but in the nineteenth and twentieth centuries as a result of the 'Romantic revolution'. Blomfield descended to the level of absurdity, when he wrote that Harrison 'followed the profession more from a love of the art, and not with a view to pecuniary emoluments' – an implausible view, and one easier to hold by a man in receipt of two good salaries than by a man who is self-employed. However, he then wrote with more insight that Harrison was 'a man of great modesty and diffidence – shy, reserved and abrupt in his manner', adding that 'his personal qualities in some measure hindered his popularity with the world, and prevented him from becoming the public man which his genius and talents certainly entitled him to be'.[11]

Joseph Farington had seen much the same in 1795, when he described Harrison as 'a plain man in person and manners, with an embarrassed delivery in conversation; but very clear and ready in explaining with his pencil'.[12] Colvin put it succinctly in 1995: 'Only his isolation in Chester and a natural diffidence prevented him from becoming a national figure like Soane or Smirke'.[13] However, I cannot help thinking, with Blomfield, that 'the natural diffidence' was probably the cause, rather than the result, of 'the isolation'.

Georgian England was not a meritocratic society: birth beat talent in almost every contest, although, once talent was given patronage by people 'of birth', it could often succeed. For most of Harrison's long lifetime an architect was regarded by most clients as no more than a sort of gentlemanly tradesman, like a doctor or solicitor. Harrison was not born a gentleman and, like many talented people then, must have suffered from a lack of confidence in 'polite society', unless he were taken under the wing of a patron and offered both praise and opportunities. He was well aware of his taste and his technical skill: Cockerell noted his 'secret exultation in his fine works and his merits, but mixed with a great truth and modesty'.[14] It is clear from his letters to the Cheshire JPs in 1792 and to the Dean and Chapter in 1819 (and others) that he was both resentful at being overlooked, and also reluctant to stoop to the flattery necessary to ingratiate himself, let alone run the risk of a snub, or of making a fool of himself by claiming too much. The brothers, James and Robert Adam, who were not plagued by false modesty, were once roundly dismissed by a gentleman as 'a pair of egregious coxcombs', but they could disregard such comments, since they complemented their talents with social ease: they were the grandsons, not sons, of a builder. Their father had become, in Colvin's words, 'the leading Scottish architect of his day', and they had completed their architectural training with a study tour in Italy. So too had Harrison, of course – but at the expense of Sir Lawrence Dundas. Above all, the Adams had the confidence, which came from being gentlemen by upbringing, if not by birth. Harrison did not have this advantage, whose supreme importance then is almost impossible for us to appreciate in 2005. Perhaps too, he simply believed, as his older fellow Yorkshireman, John Carr, is reported to have said, that an architect's role was to 'arrange the necessary conveniences with some degree of art [= skill]' – that it was indeed the work of a gentlemanly tradesman, rather than of a divinely inspired artist. Harrison certainly supplied alternative designs for most of his more important commissions.

Carr's works were more varied than Harrison's, which suggests that he was a greater architect. Carr was not by birth a gentleman either, but he had an initial advantage over Harrison, since his father owned a quarry and was well known to the West Riding gentry as a designer of some competence. He started his career a couple of rungs further up the social ladder than did Harrison, and did so in his late-20s, rather than his late-30s. What is more, when Harrison returned from Rome to Yorkshire, Carr was already active there, well-regarded and accepted in County society.

Colvin mentioned what one might call Harrison's *chutzpah* in 1773 – his impetuous reluctance to submit to what he regarded as an injustice – but making a professional career in one's own country is harder than making a stir as a foreign student. No conclusive documentary evidence has come to light, but I believe that Harrison did try to start a career in London as soon as he returned from Rome in 1776, by exhibiting at the Royal Academy in 1777, following contacts and trying to make himself known through speculative designs. It was the natural thing to do – George Cuit had tried it too – but, when the building boom faltered, Harrison's contacts did not produce commissions, before his money ran out. In two awful words, he failed.

Despite the good fortune, which had taken him to Rome, Harrison had to wait ten long years to secure some recognition. It took him another ten years to make his name in Lancaster and then Chester, but his reputation in Lancaster was a mixed one, and, when he moved to Chester, he had turned 50 and was, quite simply, overwhelmed with work – as Appendix C shows. He must have been disappointed to learn that there were trained architects in Liverpool and Manchester, as well as craftsmen armed with the books of Gibbs, Batty Langley and Nicholson. He was undoubtedly confident in 1800 that he was more than just a competent architect and that his best works had considerable quality; but there was, then just as now, a certain metropolitan arrogance, which it needs the unthinking self-confidence of youth to challenge.

Harrison probably feared that, as a family man in his mid-50s, he did not have the energy, the financial resources and, above all, the aristocratic contacts to try his luck in London again, competing this time not merely against such established figures of his own generation as Dance, Holland, Soane and Wyatt, but also against ambitious and well connected young men, like Smirke and Wilkins. It was not absolutely necessary in Georgian England to establish oneself in London to enjoy a successful career and something like a national reputation: Carr and both the John Woods in Bath had proved the point. Success in London would have brought him greater wealth and, perhaps, some fame, but a second failure would have meant a life of draftsman's drudgery. I surmise, in conclusion, that he felt that he could find enough work to do in and around Chester and decided that, by staying there and relying on the almost automatic patronage of wealthy merchants, professional men and local gentry, who recognised his competence, he had found his best niche in the society of Regency England – as a fairly big fish in a fairly small pool.

* * *

That is sad, perhaps, in our post-Romantic eyes, but Harrison was born in 1744, not 1944. I think, though, that it was an accurate self-assessment. Harrison was a historically significant English architect, certainly the most important north-western architect of his day, but not quite a major one in national terms.[*] He helped to introduce the Greek Revival, but, although every one of his surviving buildings is listed, he produced only half a dozen really great buildings – buildings which strike one's eyes, then satisfy one's mind and lastly remain long in one's memory.

Cockerell, even though he had probably not seen either of the Shire Halls or the Lyceum or the Portico Library, was right to assess that Harrison's exteriors were generally finer than his interiors. Harrison was seldom commissioned to design buildings which needed memorable interiors or even a coherent suite of fine and varied internal spaces. On the other hand, many of his monuments and exteriors are undoubtedly grand. Several, like the Shire Hall at Lancaster, the Propylaea Gateway at Chester and Hawkstone Citadel, compose well as three-dimensional masses of stonework, while a few present two contrasting façades to be seen in one diagonal view. However, his best works are not large complexes with complicated relationships between their masses, but are, rather, free-standing buildings on a fairly small scale. This is not a criticism: Harrison

---

[*] Too much has been made of Richard Cumberland's appraisal that 'when the modest genius of a Harrison shall be brought into fuller display, England will have to boast of a native architect, which the brightest age of Greece would glory to acknowledge'. Cumberland was a playwright and journalist and made his comment in 1791 in a wide-ranging essay on English culture, in which he made the debatable claim that, as regards her painters and sculptors, England 'stands without a rival' [in Europe]. He was also a friend of the Kendal artist, George Romney, and may therefore have met Harrison. However, in 1791 the only designs by Harrison, which he could have seen, were those exhibited at the Royal Academy and the early buildings at Lancaster. Cumberland's comment is no more than a prediction, based on a (justifiable) enthusiasm for Skerton Bridge and the Piazza del Popolo; it has little value as an assessment of Harrison's work as a whole.

had few chances – as it were – to compose symphonies, but he wrote many string quartets; and in them he was second to few in his heydey.

* * *

Harrison chose not to go to London again. If, however, he had gone there in 1800, against his assessment of the odds, and made a successful career – stimulated to new ideas by the challenge of talented rivals – the quality of a few of his later buildings suggest that our national architectural heritage might well have been richer; but who knows that he would have obtained good commissions? If, though, he had gone to London and failed, his Propylaea Gateway and Grosvenor Bridge in Chester would not have been built; and for this – wherever we live – we should be pleased.

Writing 'what-if?' history is fun but futile, so I shall conclude with an opinion, based on real buildings. The architectural quality of a dozen of Thomas Harrison's buildings, not to mention the historical importance of others in the introduction of the Greek Revival, give him a significant place in the story of English architecture and make a detour to see some of these works in and around Chester, Lancaster, Liverpool and Manchester well worth the effort, two centuries after he practised.

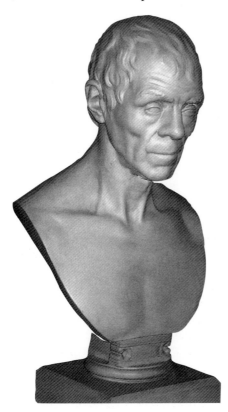

Thomas Harrison (1744–1829)

References

Introduction

1. N. Pevsner & E. Hubbard, *The Buildings of England: Cheshire* (1971) p. 29.
2. J. Summerson, *Architecture in Britain 1530–1830* (1991), p. 432 and p. 434.
3. D. Watkin *English Architecture, a concise history* (1997), p. 149.
4. D. Watkin *The Buildings of Britain: Regency* (1982), p. 190.
5. H. Colvin, *Biographical Dictionary of British Architects 1600–1840* (1995), pp. 466–70.
6. J. Mordaunt Crook, 'The architecture of Thomas Harrison', *Country Life* 15 April, 22 April and 6 May 1971.
7. M.A.R. Ockrim, 'The Life and Work of Thomas Harrison of Chester' (unpublished Ph.D. thesis, Courtauld Institute of Art, London, 1988).
8. *Oxford Dictionary of National Biography* (2004) vol 25, pp. 535–7.

Chapter 1: Origins and Training

1. Much of the information on Harrison's life in Richmond came from Jane Hatcher.
2. Cheshire Record Office, CR 73/1–4.
3. Cheshire RO, CR 73/19.
4. C.R.Cockerell, unpublished diary entry, July 1818, quoted in M. Ockrim, Thesis, p. 51.
5. H. Colvin, *Dictionary*, p. 466.
6. Cheshire RO, Z.CR 73/20.

Chapter 2: Skerton Bridge

1. A. Skempton (ed) *Biographical Dictionary of Civil Engineers in Great Britain and Ireland* (2002) vol I, pp. 771–3.
2. H. Colvin, *Dictionary*. p. 419.
3. Lancashire Record Office, QAR 2/5.
4. Lancaster Borough Records, *Minutes Book 1765–94*, p. 213.
5. Lancashire RO, QAR 5/30.
6. Lancaster Library, A. Hewitson, *Memoranda*, (no date) vol. II, p. 334.
7. C.Clark, *An Account of Lancaster* (1807), p. 43.
8. Quoted in A.White (ed) *History of Lancaster, 1193–1993* (1993), p. 119.
9. Victoria & Albert Museum Prints & Drawings Collection, WD 64 (i).

Chapter 3: Other Early Bridges

1. Derby City Library, BA711.
2. Derbyshire County Record Office, Harrington papers, D518 M/Z 1–2.
3. A.Taylor, 'Thomas Harrison and the Stramongate Bridge, Kendal' in *Trans. Cumberland and Westmorland Antiq. and Arch. Soc.* (1969), pp. 275–9.
4. A.Taylor, *The Websters of Kendal: A North-Western Architectural Dynasty* (2004), p. 165.
5. Lancashire Record Office, QSO/2/161.
6. Lancashire RO, QAR 6.
7. Lancashire RO, QSO/2/162.
8. Cheshire Record Office, CR 73/53.

Chapter 4: Other Works in Lancaster

1. Andrew White (*pers. comm.*).
2. Lancaster Borough Records, *Minutes Book 1765–94*, pp. 255, 266 and 317.
3. H. Colvin, *Dictionary,* p. 39.
4. Lancashire Record Office, QAL 1/1(3.10.1786).
5. Lancaster Borough Records, *Minutes Book 1756–9,* p. 305 and p. 320.
6. Lancaster BR, *Minutes,* p. 243.
7. George Howson (*pers. comm.*).
8. E. Twycross, *Mansions of England and Wales: Lancaster* (1846), vol. II, p. 21.
9. Lancaster City Museum, Lan 96. 45/684.
10. W. Farrer & J. Brownbill, *The Victoria County History of Lancaster,* vol. 8 (1914), p. 34.
11. A. Hewitson, *Northwards,* (1900) p.152.
12. 'Cross Fleury', *Time-honoured Lancaster* (1891), p. 574.
13. E. Twycross, *Mansions* (1846), vol. II, p. 21.
14. Dorothy Simpson (*pers. comm.*).

Chapter 5: Lancaster and Chester Castles

1. Lancashire Record Office, QAL 1/1.
2. M. Ockrim, Thesis (1988), pp. 74 and 75.
3. Cheshire Record Office, QAB 1/1.
4. Quoted in M. Ockrim, Thesis, p. 90.
5. C. Clark, *An Account of Lancaster* (1807), between pp. 16 and 17.
6. G. Worsley, *Classical Architecture in Britain: the Heroic Age* (1995), p. 306.
7. Eric Wilkinson spoke with the repairs craftsmen in 2000 (*pers. comm.*).
8. Lancashire RO, QAL 1/1 (14 April 1794).
9. C. Clark, Account, p. 28.
10. Nine of the Freebairn paintings can be seen in J. Champness, *Lancaster Castle: A Brief History* (1993).
11. *The Times* (4 September 1816, p. 3, col. C).
12. Cheshire RO, QAB 2/2/3.
13. Cheshire Museums Service, CMS. 1977.3419.
14. N. Pevsner & E. Hubbard, *Buildings of England: Cheshire*, p.157.
15. H. Colvin, Dictionary, p. 466.

16. Quoted in G. Darley, *John Soane: an accidental Romantic* (1999), p. 199.
17. C. Cockerell, diary entries for 9 November 1823 and 4 March 1828, quoted in M. Ockrim, Thesis, p. 388.

Chapter 6: Thomas Harrison 'of Chester'
1. H. Colvin, *Dictionary*, p. 998.
2. H. Colvin, *Dictionary*, p. 45.
3. Quoted in H. Colvin, *Dictionary*, p. 45.
4. The Countess of Wemyss (*pers. comm.*).
5. H. Colvin, *Dictionary*, p. 465.
6. H. Colvin, *Dictionary*, pp. 265–6.

Chapter 7: Country Houses
1. A. White, *Lancaster: A History* (2003), p.121.
2. The Countess of Wemyss (*pers. comm.*).
3. Cheshire Museums Service, 1977.2860.
4. The Countess of Wemyss (*pers. comm.*).
5. The Countess of Wemyss (*pers. comm.*).
6. This plan appears on the front endpapers of B. Wragg and G. Worsley, *The Life and Works of John Carr* (2000).
7. M. Ockrim, Thesis, pp. 112–145.
8. In a letter of thanks to the antiquarian, William Hamilton, who had proposed him for membership of the Society of Dilettanti: The Earl of Elgin (*pers. comm.*).
9. The Earl of Elgin (*pers.comm.*).
10. The Earl of Elgin (*pers. comm.*).
11. H. Colvin, 'The beginnings of the architectural profession in Scotland', *Architectural History* (1986).
12. H. Colvin, *Dictionary*, pp. 279–80.
13. J. Gifford, C. McWilliam & D. Walker, *The Buildings of Scotland – Edinburgh* (1984), p. 516.
14. Mike Derbyshire (*pers. comm.*).
15. George Howson and Pam Bosworth (*pers. comm.*).
16. John Martin Robinson (*pers. comm.*).

Chapter 8 – Liverpool and Manchester
1. J. Farington, *Diary*, 22 September 1808.
2. A. Brooks & B. Howarth, *Boomtown Manchester* (1993), p. 19.
3. C. Stewart, *The Stones of Manchester* (1956), p.18.

Chapter 9: Churches
1. Shropshire Archives, P 305/B/3/1/1.
2. J. Hanshall, *History of the County Palatine of Chester* (1817), pp. 398–9.
3. Cheshire Record Office, CR 73/25–40.
4. Cheshire RO, EDD 4/4.

Chapter 10: Later Works

1. The story is told more fully in F. Maddox, *Chester City Club: an Historical Sketch* (second edition 1990).
2. E. Hubbard, *The Buildings of Wales: Clwyd* (2001), p. 362.
3. M. Ockrim, Thesis, pp. 112–45.
4. Cheshire Record Office, CR 73/51.
5. C. Cockerell, Diary for 9 November 1823, quoted in M. Ockrim, Thesis, p. 314.
6. P. Cannon-Brookes, *Tabley House* (1991), p. 19.
7. R. Newcome, *Account of the Castle and Town of Denbigh* (1829), pp. 124–5.
8. E. Hubbard, *Clwyd* (2001), p.148.
9. J. Williams *Ancient and Modern Denbigh* (1856).
10. G. Ormerod, *History of the County Palatine and City of Chester* (2nd edition, 1882), *vol I, p. 586.*
11. E. Twycross, *The Mansions of England and Wales – Cheshire* (1850), vol II, p. 127.
12. Iain Sharp (*pers. comm.*).
13. J. Hemingway, *History of the City of Chester* (1831), vol I, p. 429.
14. E. Baines, *History, Directory and Gazetteer of the County Palatine of Lancaster* (1825), vol. II, p. 699.
15. R. Stewart Brown. *History of the Manor and Township of Allerton* (1911), p 185.
16 P. Fleetwood-Hesketh, *Murray's Lancashire Architectural Guide* (1955) p. 93.
17. National Monuments Record, drawing E/46/86, illustrated in M. Ockrim, Thesis, plate 4.42.
18. D. Watkin, *Life and Work of C. R. Cockerell* (1974) p. 70.

Chapter 11: Monuments

1. The story is more fully told in P. Howell, 'The Jubilee Tower on Moel Fammau', *Architectural History* (1984).
2. H. Colvin, *Dictionary,* (1995), p. 479.
3. M. Ockrim, 'Thomas Harrison and "the Structural Department of the Art"', *Georgian Group Journal* (1992), p. 75.
4. The story is more fully told in Marquess of Anglesey, *The First Marquess of Anglesey's Column* (1957).
5. Cheshire Record Office, QAB1/11.
6. The story is more fully told in E. Parry, *Royal Visits and Progresses in Wales* (1850), pp. 419–26.

Chapter 12 – Last Houses

1. Chester Heritage Centre, Z 26/1.
2. P. De Figuereido & J. Treuherz, *Cheshire Country Houses* (1988) p. 179.
3. Quoted in M. Hall, 'Chirk Castle, Denbighshire', *Country Life* (16 July 1992) p. 54.
4. P. Reid, *Burke's and Savill's Guide to Country Houses*, vol. II (1980) p. 91.
5. Shropshire Archives, PH/H/7.
6. The story is more fully told in H. Colvin, *Unbuilt Oxford*, (1983), pp. 81–85.
7. H. Colvin, *Dictionary*, pp. 736–7.

8. The drawings can also be seen in R. White, *The Architectural Drawings of Magdalen College,* Oxford (2001), pp. 91–98.

9. The contract in the Magdalen College archives (MC:FA14/4/5L1) refers to Parkinson's designs: Dr Robin Darwall-Smith (*pers. comm.*).

10. J. Mordaunt Crook, 'The Architecture of Thomas Harrison' *Country Life* (15 April 1971), p. 876.

11. C. Cockerell, Diary for 9 November 1823, quoted in M. Ockrim Thesis, p. 177.

Chapter 13: Cheshire Bridges
1. Cheshire Record Office, QJB 3/19, 3/20 and 3/21.

2. Cheshire RO, QJB 3/20, p. 375.

3. The specification is in Cheshire RO, QAR/18 (23 November 1812).

4. Warrington Library, MS 36, pp. 68 and 78.

5. E. Baines. *History, Directory and Gazetteer of the County Palatine of Lancaster* (1825), vol. II, p. 582.

6. J. Hanshall, *History of the County Palatine of Chester* (1817), p. 598.

7. Cheshire RO, TRB/176–189.

8. The story is told more fully in J. Clarke, 'The Building of the Grosvenor Bridge', *Trans. Chester & N. Wales Arch. Soc.* XLV (1958).

9. Cheshire RO, TRB 166.

10. Quoted in H. Colvin, *Dictionary* (1995), p. 992.

11. J. Mordaunt Crook, 'The Architecture of Thomas Harrison', *Country Life* (6 May 1971), p. 1088.

Conclusion: The Significance of Thomas Harrison
1. National Portrait Gallery, D 13554; an actual copy of the print is in the Cheshire Record Office, VPR.

2. Quoted in M.Ockrim,Thesis, p. 330.

3. J. Hemingway, *History of the City of Chester* (1831), pp. 362–4.

4. I have found mentions of Harrison in London in the summer of 1786, in February 1787, December 1795, at the sale of Chambers' library in July 1796, in March 1797, April 1799 and in July 1818.

5. Cockerell's Diary for 9 November 1823, quoted in M. Ockrim, Thesis, p. 314.

6. Cockerell's Diary for 4 March 1828, quoted in M. Ockrim, Thesis, p. 388.

7. Cockerell's Diary for 9 November 1823, quoted in M. Ockrim, Thesis, p. 314.

8. H. Colvin, *Dictionary* (1995), p. 467.

9. D. Watkin, *English Architecture – a Concise History* (1997), p. 149.

10. G. Worsley, *Architectural Drawings of the Regency Period* (1991), p. 40.

11. G. Blomfield, 'Harrison of Chester, Architect', *The Builder* (21 March 1863), pp. 203–5

12. J. Farington, Diary for 20 December 1795, quoted in H. Colvin, *Dictionary,* p. 467.

13. H. Colvin, *Dictionary,* p. 467.

14. Cockerell's Diary for 9 November 1823, quoted in M. Ockrim, Thesis, p. 314.

APPENDIX A

Chronological List of Harrison's Known Works, including significant unbuilt designs

The numbers in the margin are those used in Appendix C, which attempts to show Harrison's workload in diagrammatic form.

The first date given is the date of the design, the second the date of completion; in many cases one or other of these dates is only approximate.

Buildings, whose names are printed *in italics*, were built, but have been demolished.
Those whose names are printed in **bold type** can be certainly attributed to Harrison.
Those which are <u>underlined</u> are almost certainly by him.
Those in normal type are only probably by him.
Buildings whose names are printed in CAPITALS are, in my view, the most significant of Harrison's works, in terms of historical interest or architectural quality.

1. **1782–87. LANCASTER – SKERTON BRIDGE (97/47.62)**

2. **1782–83. Lancaster – Town Hall (now City Museum) clock tower**

3. 1783–84. Lancaster – St John's Chapel tower and spire

4. 1786–87. Lancaster – Bridge Houses

5. **1786–1801. CHESTER – COUNTY GAOL** (largely demolished)

6. **1787–96. LANCASTER – COUNTY GAOL**

7. 1788–93. Derby – St Mary's Bridge

8. **1789–90.** *Sawley – Harrington Bridge* **(129/47.31)**

9. 1790–92. <u>*Lancaster – Springfield Hall*</u>

10. **1791–94.** Kendal – Stramongate Bridge

11. 1793. <u>GOSFORD, EAST LOTHIAN – MAUSOLEUM</u> (66/45.78)

12. **1793–95.** *KENNETT HOUSE, Clackmannan* **(58/92.90)**

13. *c.*1793. Lonsdale bridges – (Cocker Bridge (102/45.51)), Denny Beck Bridge (97/50.64) and Mill House Bridge (102/43.50)

14. **1794–1802.** CHESTER – SHIRE HALL

15. 1795–98. <u>Quernmore Park Hall</u> (97/51.62) and its Chain Lodge (97/51.64)

16. **1795–99.** Broomhall, Fife **(65/07.83)**

17. **1796–98.** LANCASTER – SHIRE HALL, Crown Court and Grand Jury Room.

18. *c.***1800.** Cheshire bridges – Lindford bridge **(118/91.65)**, Oversley Ford bridge **(109/81.82)** and Radnor bridge **(118/83.65)**

19. **1800–02.** LIVERPOOL – LYCEUM_

20. **1801.** *Middlewich, House of Correction*

21. **1801–02.** Colinton House, near Edinburgh **(66/21.69)**

22. **1802–06.** MANCHESTER, PORTICO LIBRARY

23. **1802–06.** Whittington, Shropshire – St John the Baptist **(126/32.31)**

24. *c.***1804.** Lowther Hall (designs)

25. **1804.** Chester – St Peter – refacing south wall

26. **1804–10.** Chester – Castle Armoury and Barracks

27.   1805. Carlisle – Eden Bridge (designs)

28.   *1805–09. Manchester – Exchange*

29.   *1806–07. Manchester – Theatre Royal*

30.   *1806–08. Chester – City Gaol and House of Correction*

31.   1807–08. Chester – Commercial News Room (now City Club)

32.   *1807–11. Gredington House, Flintshire* (**126/44.38**)

33.   1808–10. CHESTER, NORTH GATE

34.   *c.*1808–10. TABLEY HOUSE, PICTURE GALLERY
      (**118/72.77**)

35.   1808–15. CHESTER – PROPYLAEA GATEWAY AT THE
      CASTLE

36.   1810–13. Denbigh – Infirmary (**116/06.66**)

37.   c.1810. Oughtrington Hall, Cheshire (109/69.87)

38.   1810–15. LIVERPOOL – ST NICHOLAS' STEEPLE

39.   1811. Chester – Wesleyan Methodist Church (much rebuilt)

40.   *1811–13. Jubilee Tower on Moel Fammau, Denbighshire*
      (**116/16.62**)

41.   1812–14. WOODBANK, STOCKPORT (109/91.90)

42.   c.1812. Glan-yr-Afon, near Loggerheads (116/19.61)

43.   *1812–17. Warrington – Mersey Bridge*

44.   1813. Chester – St Peter – refacing tower

45.   1814. Chester – Dee Hills

46.   1814–16. SHREWSBURY – LORD HILL'S COLUMN
      (**126/50.12**)

47. **1814–16.** *High Legh chapel* (totally rebuilt after a fire 1891) (109/70.84)

48. **1815–16.** *Cranage Bridge*

49. 1815-16. <u>ALLERTON – GROVE HOUSE</u> (gutted 1944) (108/41.86)

50. **1816–7.** Llanfairpwll – The Anglesey Column (114/53.71)

51. **1818.** *Liverpool – St Paul – domed ceiling*

52. **1818–25.** Chester – Old Dee Bridge widening

53. **1819.** Chester – Cathedral – designs for repairs

54. **1820–21.** CHESTER – WATERGATE HOUSE

55. **c.1820.** *Chester – Exchange – internal alterations*

56. **c.1820.** Chirk Castle – east wing (126/26.38)

57. **c.1820.** *Hoole House – conservatory* (117/43.68)

58. **1821–26.** Tilstone Lodge (117/56.61)

59. **1821–24.** *Hardwick Grange, Shropshire* (126/52.21)

60. **1821–24.** OXFORD – MAGDALEN COLLEGE – completion of the New Building and CLASSICAL DESIGN FOR THE NEW GREAT QUADRANGLE

61. **1822–23.** CHESTER – ST MARTIN'S LODGE

62. **1822–24.** HOLYHEAD – MEMORIAL GATEWAY (114/25.82)

63. **1823.** Vorontsov Palace (designs)

64. **1824–25.** HAWKSTONE CITADEL (126/57.28)

65. **1824–33.** CHESTER – GROSVENOR BRIDGE

Designs by Harrison, which were not built

Like all architects, Harrison designed schemes, which were either not related to a commission or never implemented for one reason or another. Some were speculative, others were fantasies, created with no thoughts of the constraints of a client's wishes, and I have mentioned a few of these in Chapters 1, 3 and 11. Others again were more seriously intended, drawn in response to a commission, but not accepted by the client.

Of these the most interesting are the several plans, which he drew in 1804 for the rebuilding of Lowther Hall in Westmorland. Ockrim (Thesis, pp.167–70 and 185–88) describes them at some length. It was a difficult commission, since the new building had to stand between the existing stables and kitchens, but had also to allow views from the house down the beautiful Lowther valley. Harrison produced designs in both the Classical and the Gothick manners. For the former he used some of his ideas from Broomhall and the Shire Halls and some derived from Robert Adam's work – notably in the varied plans of rooms with large niches or screens of columns in front of apses. His Gothick designs were detailed as castles or as cloisters, but, apart from the entrance hall and saloon, were decorated with fashionable Classical motifs. If some of these designs had been built, they would have provided some interesting spaces and sequences of rooms, but the need to embrace the view down the valley led to long corridors and diagonal axes, and I doubt that any of his designs would have resulted in a house convenient for living or entertaining. None was in fact accepted, and the present Lowther Castle was built to the designs of Robert Smirke.

Ockrim (Thesis, p. 344) also relates that in February 1805, perhaps because he was visiting Westmorland, Harrison was asked for advice, plans and an estimate for a new Eden Bridge at Carlisle. It is clear that he visited the site – he was paid £10 for 'attending' – but he did not reply until July – which was too late for the County's JPs. He suggested five equal semi-elliptical arches of 60 feet span with piers decorated by niches – rather like Skerton Bridge – and three smaller arches on the south abutment. Smirke also won that commission.

Harrison was not asked to compete in 1809 in the competition to design a new London Bridge, but he was asked for comments on the winning design, produced by the engineer, George Dodd. He criticised the design, on the grounds that it was little more than a copy of Perronet's famous bridge at Neuilly, and also sent a couple of his own drawings, one of which is perhaps now in the collection of the Cheshire Museums Service (1977.3419.8b); the design is derived from Skerton Bridge, but has stop-fluted Doric columns on the cutwaters and a central span of 110 feet. In the event Dodd's design was replaced by one from John Rennie, which too was perhaps loosely derived from Skerton Bridge.

In 1810 Harrison's advice was sought about the old Ouse Bridge at York. He recommended the building of a new bridge and then served as an assessor in the competition, which was won by Peter Atkinson.

Colvin (*Dictionary*, p. 469) and Ockrim (Thesis, pp. 184–5) also mention Harrison's designs for an enormous palace on the banks of the Dnieper near its mouth in the Ukraine. (These plans are now thought to have been drawn for a palace in Odessa.) They were made in about 1823 for the Count Michael Vorontsov, who was the son of a former Russian Ambassador to Great Britain. A couple of Harrison's drawings, which are in the Chester County Record Office (CR 73/24) and the Grosvenor Museum (1952.96), show a somewhat muddled entrance façade with a tall Corinthian portico in front of the two-and-a-half-storey central block. This is linked by Doric colonnades to the two-storey side wings, which flank the entrance courtyard. The sides of these wings, facing on to the courtyard, have free-standing Doric porticos, while the centres of the forward-facing façades of these wings are emphasised by Doric half-columns. If the design was ever built, it was only after significant alterations.

Harrison's Workload

If ones plots on a bar-chart information, year by year, about the dates of the commission and the completion of Harrison's schemes – using as 'building blocks' the numbers in Appendix A – one arrives at a rough indication of his workload at any time of his career. It cannot be more precise, since precise dates are seldom available.

If one assumes that more mental effort is involved in designing a building than in supervising its construction – printing design work in italics on a dark background – the chart shows clearly that in most years after 1789 Harrison had at least five jobs in progress, and that almost every year saw him involved in design work. There were peaks in the mid 1790s, when he was involved with the two castles but also with some country houses; around the turn of the centuries, when he was also working in Liverpool and Manchester; then for most of the 12 years between 1804 and 1816, when his career in Chester flourished; and finally in the early 1820s with more small country houses. It becomes easier to understand both his problems in Lancaster before 1795, and also why after that he never tried his luck again in London: he had quite enough to do in Chester.

Harrison's Annual Workload 1782—1826

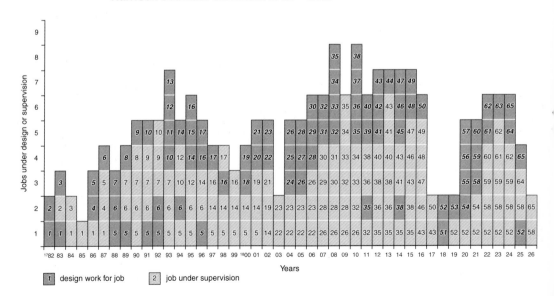

Index

Occasional Papers from the Centre for North-West Regional Studies

The Centre for North-West Regional Studies, based at Lancaster University, brings together members of the University and the regional community. As well as its extensive publication programme of Occasional Papers and Resource Papers, the Centre organises conferences, study days and seminars covering a wide range of subjects. For a small annual subscription 'Friends of the Centre' receive regular mailings of events and discounts on books and other activities

For further details contact Centre for North-West Regional Studies, Fylde College, Lancaster University, Lancaster LA1 4YF
Tel: 01524 593770; Fax: 01524 594725
Email: christine.wilkinson@lancaster.ac.uk   Website: www.lancs.ac.uk/users/cnwrs/

Thomas Harrison, Georgian Architect of Chester and Lancaster, 1744–1829 (2005) John Champness, £12.50
Romans and Briton in North West England (third revised and extended edition) (2004) David Shotter, £13.50
Stained Glass from Shrigley and Hunt of Lancaster and London (2003) William Waters, £26.95
Transforming Fell and Valley (2003) Ian Whyte, £11.50
Walking Roman Roads in Lonsdale and the Eden Valley (2002) Philip Graystone, £10.95
The Wray Flood of 1967 (2002) Emmeline Garnett, £10.95
A Fylde Country Practice (2001) Steen King, £10.95
Irish Women in Lancashire (2001) Sharon Lambert, £9.95
Hadrian's Wall: A Social and Cultural History (2000) Alison Ewin, £8.50
Furness Abbey: Romance, Scholarship and Culture (2000) Christine Dade-Robertson, £11.50
Rural Industries of the Lune Valley (2000) ed. Michael Winstanley, £9.95
The Romans at Ribchester (2000) B. J. N. Edwards £8.95
The Buildings of Georgian Lancaster (revised edition) (2000) Andrew White £6.95
A History of Linen in the North West (1998) ed. Elizabeth Roberts, £6.95
History of Roman Catholicism in the Furness Peninsula (1998) Anne C. Parkinson, £6.95
Vikings in the North West – The Artifacts (1998) B. J. N. Edwards, £6.95
Sharpe, Paley and Austin, A Lancaster Architectural Practice 1836–1952 (1998) James Price, £6.95
Victorian Terraced Housing in Lancaster (1996) Andrew White and Mike Winstanley, £6.95
Walking Roman Roads in the Fylde and the Ribble Valley (1996) Philip Graystone, £5.95
Romans in Lonsdale (1995) David Shotter and Andrew White, £6.50
Roman Route Across the Northern Lake District, Brougham to Moresby (1994) Martin Allan, £5.95
Walking Roman Roads in East Cumbria (1994) Philip Graystone, £5.95
St Martin's College, Lancaster, 1964–89 (1993) Peter S. Gedge and Lois M. R. Louden, £5.95
From Lancaster to the Lakes: the Region in Literature (1992) eds Keith Hanley and Alison Millbank, £5.95
Windermere in the Nineteenth Century (1991) ed. Oliver M. Westall, £4.95
Richard Marsden and the Preston Chartists (1981) J. E. King, £3.95

Each of these titles may be ordered by post from the above address. Postage and packing is £1.00 per order. Please make cheques payable to 'The University of Lancaster'. Titles are also available from all good booksellers in the region.